COLONIAL RECORDS

OF

VIRGINIA.

CLEARFIELD COMPANY
REPRINTS & REMAINDERS

Originally Published As
Senate Document—*Extra*
Richmond, 1874

Reprinted
Genealogical Publishing Co., Inc.
Baltimore, 1964

Reissued
Genealogical Publishing Co., Inc.
Baltimore, 1973

This Reprint Published by
Clearfield Company
Baltimore, MD
1992

Reprinted for Clearfield Company Inc. by
Genealogical Publishing Co. Inc.

Library of Congress Catalogue Card Number 73-5104
International Standard Book Number 0-8063-0558-4

Made in the United States of America

CONTENTS.

ERRATA.

Page 13—Note 50.—For McDowell read McDonald.

Page 14.—In last line of notes insert comma after Bancroft.

Page 23.—Omit the whole of note 263.

Page 24.—Note, 287, should read: committees, McDonald.

Page 35.—In second line from bottom for Stith read Smith.

Page 41 and 50.—For I, in notes, read we.

Page 61.—In Editor's Note, for Neil read Neill.

Page iii.—In Preface to Brief Declaration, lines fourteen and seventeen, for Smythe read Smith.

Page iii.—*Ib.*, line 29, for Kieth read Keith.

Page iv.—Line twenty-one, for Forcer read Force's.

Page 89.—Preface, line eight, omit "the" before massacre.

THE PROCEEDINGS

OF THE

FIRST ASSEMBLY OF VIRGINIA,

Held July 30th, 1619.

INTRODUCTION.

The documents herewith presented are printed from copies obtained from the Public Record Office of Great Britian. When the question of the boundary line between Maryland and Virginia was before the Legislature of the latter State, in 1860, Colonel Angus W. McDonald was sent to England to obtain the papers necessary to protect the interests of Virginia. He brought back " nine volumes of manuscripts and one book containing forty-eight maps" (see his report, Virginia Legislative Documents, No. 39, 1861,)· The volumes of manuscripts contained, upon an average, 425 pages each, and were filled with valuable historical documents, of many of which no copies had ever been seen on this continent since the originals were sent from the Colony of Virginia. In a conversation with the writer, held soon after his return from England, in March, 1861, Colonel McDonald stated that having obtained copies of all the documents relating to the question of the boundary line which could be found, and having more money left of the appropriation made than was needed to pay the expenses of his return home, he decided to devote the surplus to obtaining copies of papers relating to the early history of the State, without reference to the question of the boundary line. This statement will, we presume, satisfactorily account for the presence in his collection of such papers as do not relate to the subject upon which he was engaged. That he was well qualified to select such papers is evident from an examination of the list which he made out.

During the occupation of the State capitol building by the Federal troops and officials, after the surrender of the Confederate authorities in April, 1865, a very large quantity of the official documents filed in the archives of the State were removed from that building, and at the same time four of the nine volumes and the portfolio of maps above mentioned. Nothing has been heard from any of them since. In 1870, the question of the boundary line being again before the Legislature of Virginia, the Governor sent the Hon. D. C. De Jarnette upon the same errand that Colonel McDonald had so well performed, and the result was the obtaining of such papers as he could find relating to the subject under consideration, including duplicates of some of those which though useful in this connection, are included in the five volumes remaining of those collected by Col. McDonald; also, charters of great length, but which are to be found in print in the histories and statutes of the State, andmany of the miscellaneous papers which Colonel McDonald had copied under the circumstances above named. Among the latter is the account of the first meeting of the Assembly at Jamestown in 1619. When Colonel McDonald visited the State Paper Office (as it was then called) in 1860, this great repository of historical materials had not been thrown open to the public, and he tells us in his report that it was "twenty days after his arrival in London before he could obtain permission to examine the archives of the State Paper Office." A year or two afterwards all of the restrictions which had existed were removed, the papers arranged chronologically, and an index made by which they could be referred to. Farther, W. Noel Sainsbury, Esq., one of the officers of what is now called the Public Record Office, had published a calendar of all the papers relating to the British colonies in North America and the West Indies, from the first discoveries to 1660 (soon be followed by another coming down to the period of the independence of the United States), which contains a brief abstract of every paper included in the above named period, so that enquirers upon subjects embraced in this calendar can by reference see what the office has on file relating to it, and obtain copies of the documents required, at a much less cost than a voyage to England. Acting upon this knowledge, the Library Committee of the Virginia Legislature has made a contract with Mr. Sainsbury for copies of the titles and copious abstracts of every paper in the Public Record Office, and other repositories, which relates to the history of Virginia while a Colony. All of which he proposes to furnish for about £250, being less than one-half the cost of either of the missions sent, which have obtained only a small fraction of the papers which we are to receive. He is performing his work in a most satisfactory manner; so much is he interested in the task that he has greatly exceeded his agreement by furnishing gratuitously full and complete copies of many documents of more than ordinary interest. Yet notwithstanding the known facilities afforded by the British Government and its officials, Mr. De Jarnette complains that he was refused permission to examine the Rolls Office and the State Paper Office (see his report, Senate Documents Session 1871-'2, p. 12); and further, on page 15, he informs us that the papers which he obtained "had to be dug from a mountain of Colonial records with care and labor." His troubles were further increased by the fact that "the Colonial papers are not arranged under heads of respective Colonies, but thrown promiscuously together and constitute an immense mass of ill kept and badly written records," ib. p. 22.

The reader will infer from the preceding remarks that the State has two complete copies of the record of the proceedings of the first Assembly which met at Jamestown, viz: the McDonald and the De Jarnette copies, and also an abstract furnished by Mr. Sainsbury. Bancroft, the historian, obtained a copy of this paper, which was printed in the collections of the New York Historical Society for 1857. We have therefore been enabled to compare three different versions, and in a measure, a fourth. The De Jarnette copy being in loose sheets, written on one side only, was selected as the most convenient for the printer, and the text is printed from it. Where this differs from either of the others the foot notes show the differences, and when no reference is made it is because all of them correspond.

When these papers were submitted as a part of the report of the Commissioners on the Boundary Line a joint resolution was adopted by both houses of the Legislature authorizing the Committee on the Library to print such of the papers as might be selected, provided the consent of the Commission could be obtained. Application was made to allow the first and second papers in this pamphlet to be printed but it was refused. The Commission having been dissolved the Committee on the Library have assumed the responsibility and herewith submit this instalment of these interesting documents, which were written before the Colony of Maryland was known, and all of which, save the first, were never before printed.

The Report of the proceedings of the first Assembly is prefaced with the introductory note published with Mr. Bancroft's copy, to which a few notes explanatory have been added.

Trusting that this instalment of these historical records of the Ancient Dominion will be acceptable to the students of our early history, and sufficiently impress the members of the Legislature with their value to move them to make an appropriation sufficient to print all that has been obtained, this is

Respectfully submitted,

by your obedient servants,

THOS. H. WYNNE,
Chm. Senate Com. on Library, } *Sub Committee in*
W. S. GILMAN, *Charge of Library.*
Chm. House Com. on Library.

INTRODUCTORY NOTE.

Virginia, for twelve years after its settlement, languished under the government of Sir Thomas Smith, Treasurer of the Virginia Company in England. The Colony was ruled during that period by laws written in blood; and its history shows how the narrow selfishness of despotic power could counteract the best efforts of benevolence. The colonists suffered an extremity of distress too horrible to be described.

In April, 1619, Sir George Yeardley arrived. Of the emigrants who had been sent over at great cost, not one in twenty then remained alive. "In James Citty were only those houses that Sir Thomas Gates built in the tyme of his government, with one wherein the Governor allwayes dwelt, and a church, built wholly at the charge of the inhabitants of that citye, of timber, being fifty foote in length and twenty foot in breadth." At Henrico, now Richmond, there were no more than "three old houses, a poor ruinated Church, with some few poore buildings in the Islande."[1] "For ministers to instruct the people, he founde only three authorized, two others who never received their orders." "The natives he founde uppon doubtfull termes;" so that when the twelve years of Sir Thomas Smith's government expired, Virginia, according to the "judgements" of those who were then members of the Colony, was "in a poore estate."*

From the moment of Yeardley's arrival dates the real life of Virginia. He brought with him "Commissions and instructions from the Company for the better establishinge of a Commonwealth heere."† He made proclamation, "that those cruell lawes by which we" (I use the words of the Ancient Planters themselves) "had soe longe been governed, were now abrogated, and that we were to be governed by those free lawes which his Majesties subjectes live under in Englande." Nor were these considerations made dependent on the good will of administrative officers.

"And that they might have a hande in the governinge of themselves," such are the words of the Planters, "yt was graunted that a generall Assemblie shoulde be helde yearly once, whereat were to be present the Govr and Counsell wth two Burgesses from each Plantation, freely to be elected by the Inhabitants thereof, this Assemblie to have power to make and ordaine whatsoever lawes and orders should by them be thought good and proffitable for our subsistance."‡

In conformity with these instructions, Sir George Yeardley "sente his summons all over the country, as well to invite those of the Counsell of Estate that were absente, as also for the election of Burgesses;"|| and on Friday, the 30th day of July, 1619, the first elective legislative body of this continent assembled at James City.

---

* "A Briefe Declaration of the Plantation of Virginia during the first twelve yeares, when Sir Thomas Smyth was Governor of the Companie, and downe to this present tyme. By the Ancient Planters now remaining alive in Virginia."—*MS. in my possession.*[2]

† "A Briefe Declaration," &c.

‡ "A Briefe Declaration," &c.

|| "Proceedings of the first Assembly," now first printed in this volume.

[1] "Henrico, now Richmond," is a grievous error. Henrico, or Henricus, was situated ten miles below the present site of Richmond, on the main land, to which the peninsula known as Farrar's Island was joined." See note p. 37.—ED.

[2] This document is the third in this collection. It is printed from the copy obtained by Col. McDonald.—ED.

In the relation of Master John Rolfe, inserted by Captain John Smith in his History of Virginia,* there is this meagre notice of the Assembly : " The 25 of June came in the *Triall* with Corne and Cattell in all safety, which tooke from vs cleerely all feare of famine ; then our gouernor and councell caused Burgesses to be chosen in all places, and met at a generall Assembly, where all matters were debated thought expedient. for the good of the Colony."

This account did not attract the attention of Beverley, the early historian of Virginia, who denies that there was any Assembly held there before May, 1620.†

The careful Stith, whose work is not to be corrected without a hearty recognition of his superior diligence and exemplary fidelity, gives an account‡ of this first legislative body, though he errs a little in the date by an inference from Rolfe's narrative, which the words do not warrant.

The prosperity of Virginia begins with the day when it received, as " a commonwealth," the freedom to make laws for itself. In a solemn address to King James, which was made during the government of Sir Francis Wyatt, and bears the signature of the Governor, Council, and apparently every member of the Assembly, a contrast is drawn between the former " miserable bondage," and " this just and gentle authoritye which hath cherished us of late by more worthy magistrates. And we, our wives and poor children shall ever pray to God, as our bounden duty is, to give you in this worlde all increase of happines, and to crowne you in the worlde to come wth immortall glorye."§

A desire has long existed to recover the record of the proceedings of the Assembly which inaugurated so happy a revolution. Stith was unable to find it; no traces of it were met by Jefferson; and Hening,‖ and those who followed Hening, believed it no longer extant. Indeed, it was given up as hopelessly lost.

Having, during a long period of years, instituted a very thorough research among the papers relating to America in the British State Paper Office, partly in person and partly with the assistance of able and intelligent men employed in that Department, I have at last been so fortunate as to obtain the " Proceedings of the First Assembly of Virginia."[5] The document is in the form of " a reporte " from the Speaker ; and is

---

* Smith's Generall Historie of Virginia, Richmond edition, Voll. ii, pp. 38, 39.

† See Beverley's History of Virginia, p. 37 of the first edition, and p. 35 of the second.[3]

‡ Stith's History of Virginia, p. 160, Williamsburg edition.[4]

♁ MS. Copy of Address of Sir Francis Wyatt, &c., &c., to King James I., signed by Sir Francis Wyatt and 32 others.

‖ Hening's Statutes at Large, I., p. 119, refers to the acts of 1623–'4 as " the earliest now extant."

[3] "These Burgesses met the Governor and Council at Jamestowon in 1620, and sat in consultation in the same house with them as the method of the Scots Parliament is." "This was t'.e first Generall Assembly that ever was held there."—Beverley.—Ed.

[4] " And about the latter end of June (1619) he (Sir George Yeardley, Governor,) called the first General Assembly that was ever held in Virginia. Counties were not yet laid off, but they elected their representatives by townships. So that the Burroughs of Jamestown, Henrico, Bermuda Hundred, and the rest, each sent their members to the Assembly." * * * * "and hence it is that our lower house of Assembly was first called the House of Burgesses," Stith, p. 160. " In May, this year (1620), there was held another Generall Assembly, which has, through mistake, and the indolence and negligence of our historians in searching such ancient records as are still extant in the country, been commonly reported the first General Assembly," ib. p. 182. We do not see that Stith "errs" even "a little in the date." Rolfe says, "The 25 of June came in the *Triall* with Corne and Cattell in all safety, which took from us cleerely all feare of famine, then our gouernor and councell caused Burgesses to be chosen in all places, and met at a generall Assembly," Smith, p. 126. Stith says, "And about the latter end of June he called," &c., Stith, p. 160. Neither intimate *when* the Assembly *met*, only that the governor called them in the latter part of June.—Ed.

[5] The first published notice of the existence of this paper occurred in the proceedings of the annual meeting of the Virginia Historical Society, held December 15, 1853. In the report of the Executive Committee the chairman, Conway Robinson, Esq., states that he had seen the original report in the State Paper Office in London, on a recent visit to that city.—See Virginia Historical Reporter, Vol. I, 1854. Whatever question there may be in regard to priority of discovery, it is to be regretted that it was left to the Historical Society of another State to publish a document of so much value to the one to which it solely relates.—Ed.

more full and circumstantial than any subsequent journal of early legislation in the Ancient Dominion.

Many things are noticeable. The Governor and Council sat with the Burgesses, and took part in motions and debates. The Secretary of the Colony was chosen Speaker, and I am not sure that he was a Burgess.[6] This first American Assembly set the precedent of beginning legislation with prayer. It is evident that Virginia was then as thoroughly a Church of England colony, as Connecticut afterwards was a Calvinistic one. The inauguration of legislative power in the Ancient Dominion preceded the existence of negro slavery, which we will believe it is destined also to survive. The earliest Assembly in the oldest of the original thirteen States, at its first session, took measures "towards the erecting of" a "University and Colledge." Care was also taken for the education of Indian children. Extravagance in dress was not prohibited, but the minters were to profit by a tax on excess in apparel. On the whole, the record of these Proceedings will justify the opinion of Sir Edward Sandys, that "they were very well and judiciously carried." The different functions of government may have been confounded and the laws were not framed according to any speculative theory; but a perpetual interest attaches to the first elective body representing the people of Virginia, more than a year before the Mayflower, with the Pilgrims, left the harbor of Southampton, and while Virginia was still the oldest British Colony on the whole Continent of America.

GEORGE BANCROFT.

New York, *October* 3, 1856.

[6] The Secretary of the Colony and Speaker of the first Assembly was John Pory. If he had been one of the Burgesses his name would have appeared with the others. Through the influence of the Earl of Warwick he was made Secretary to the Virginia Company. Campbell says, "He was educated at Cambridge, where he took the Master of Arts in April, 1610. It is supposed he was a member of the House of Commons. He was much of a traveller, and was at Venice in 1613, at Amsterdam in 1617, and shortly after at Paris." "Sir George Yeardley appointed him one of his Council."—Campbell, p. 139. The record shows that he acted as the presiding officer of the first Assembly, whether *ex officio* or by selection is not stated. It will be seen that a typographical error in Bancroft's pamphlet makes his name Povy. In Smith's General Historie there is a paper styled "The observations of Master John Pory, Secretarie of Virginia, in his travels;" it gives an account of his voyage to the eastern shore.—Smith, p. 141. Neill says of him, "John Pory was a graduate of Cambridge, a great traveller and good writer, but gained the reputation of being a chronic tipler and literary vagabond and sponger." When young he excited the interest of Hakluyt, who, in a dedication to the third volume of his, remarks: "Now, because long since I did foresee that my profession of Divinitie, the care of my family, and other occasions, might call or divert me from these kind of endeavour, I, therefore have, for these three years last past, encouraged and gathered in these studies of Cosmographia and former histories my honest, industrious and learned friend, Mr. John Porey, one of speciall skill and extraordinary hope, to perform great matters in the same, and beneficial to the Commonwealth." "Pory, in 1600, prepared a *Geographical History of Africa*, but he soon disappointed the expectations of his friends."

A letter from London, dated July 26, 1623, says: "Our old acquaintance, Mr. Porey, is in poore case, and in prison at the Terceras, whither he was driven by contrary winds, from the north coast of Virginia, where he had been upon some discovery, and upon his arrival he was arraigned and in danger of being hanged for a pirate." "He died about 1635." For further particulars from contemporary authorities, see Neill's History of the Virginia Company of London. Albany, Munsell, 1869.—ED.

COLONIAL RECORDS OF VIRGINIA.

STATE PAPERS.

COLONIAL.   VOL. I.—No. 45.

[July 30, 1619.]*

A REPORTE *of the manner of proceeding†* in *the General assembly convented at James citty in Virginia, July 30, 1619, consisting of the Governo*[r], *the Counsell of Estate‡ and two Burgesses elected out of eache Incorporation and Plantation, and being dissolved the 4*[th] *of August next ensuing.*

Firſt. Sir George Yeardley, Knight Governo[r] & Captaine general of Virginia, having ſente his ſumons all over the Country, as well to invite thoſe of the Counſell of Eſtate that were abſente as alſo for the election of Burgeſſes, there were choſen and appeared

> *For James citty*
> > Captaine William Powell,
> > Enſigne William Spenſe.
>
> *For Charles citty*
> > Samuel Sharpe,
> > Samuel Jordan.
>
> *For the citty of Henricus*
> > Thomas Dowſe,
> > John Polentine.

---

* The caption is after the De Jarnette copy. Bancroft has "S. P. O." (State Paper Office.) "Am'a & W. Ind. Virg.: Indorsed, Mr. Povy out of Virginia. The Proceedings of the First Assembly of Virginia: July 1619." Sainsbury's Calendar of State papers: Colonial, 1574–1660, has, "*Endorsed by Mr. Carleton.* Mr. Pory out of Virginia."—p. 22.

† Proceedings. Bancroft.   ‡ State. McDonald.

For Kiccowtan
> Captaine William Tucker,
> William Capp.

For Martin Brandon—Capt. John Martin's Pla'tation
> Mr Thomas Davis,
> Mr Robert Stacy.

For Smythe's hundred
> Captain Thomas Graves,
> Mr Walter Shelley.

For Martin's hundred
> Mr John Boys,[1]
> John Jackson.

For Argall's guiffe[2]
> Mr Pawlett,
> Mr Gourgaing.[3]

For Flowerdieu hundred
> Ensigne[4] Roffingham,
> Mr Jefferson.

For Captain Lawne's plantation
> Captain Christopher Lawne,
> Ensigne[4] Washer.

For Captaine Warde's plantation
> Captaine Warde,
> Lieutenant Gibbes.

The moſt convenient place we could finde to sitt in was the Quire of the Churche Where Sir George Yeardley, the Governour, being fett downe in his accuſtomed place, thoſe of the Counſel of Eſtate fate nexte him on both handes, excepte onely the Secretary then appointed Speaker, who fate right before him, John Twine, clerke[5] of the General aſſembly, being placed nexte the Speaker, and Thomas Pierſe, the Sergeant, ſtanding at the barre, to be ready for any ſervice the Aſſembly ſhoulde comaund[6] him. But foraſmuche as men's affaires doe little proſper where God's ſervice is neglected, all the Burgeſſes tooke their places in the Quire till a prayer was ſaid by Mr. Bucke, the Miniſter, that it would pleaſe God to guide and ſanctifie all our proceedings[7] to his owne glory and the good of this Plantation. Prayer being ended, to the intente that as we[8] had begun at God Almighty, ſo we[8] might proceed wth awful and due refpecte towards the Lieutenant, our moſt gratious and dread Soveraigne, all the Burgeſſes were intreatted to retyre themſelves into the body of the Churche, wch being done, before

---

[1] Boyes, McDonald. [2] Guifte, Bancroft. [3] Gourgainy, McDonald and Bancroft. [4] Enſign, Bancroft. [5] Clerk, McDonald. [6] Comand, McDonald. [7] Proceedinges, Bancroft. [8] wee, McDonald.

they were fully admitted, they were called in order and by name, and fo every man (none ftaggering at it) tooke the oathe of Supremacy, and then entred[9] the Affembly. At Captaine Warde the Speaker tooke exception, as at one that without any Comiffion or authority had featted himfelfe either upon the Companies, and then his Plantation would not be lawfull, or on Captain Martin's lande, and fo[10] he was but a limbe or member of him, and there could be but two Burgeffes for all. So Captaine Warde was comanded to abfente himfelfe till such time as the Affembly had agreed what was fitt for him to doe. After muche debate, they refolved on this order following:

> An order concluded by the General affembly concerning Captaine Warde, July 30th,[11] 1619, at the opening of the faid Affembly.

At the reading of the names of the Burgeffes, Exception was taken againft Captaine Warde as having planted here in Virginia without any authority or comiffion from the Trefurer, Counfell and Company in Englande. But confidering he had bene at so great chardge and paines to augmente this Colony, and had adventured his owne perfon in the action, and fince that time had brought home a good[12] quantity of fifhe, to relieve the Colony by waye of trade, and above all, becaufe the Comiffion for authorifing the General Affembly admitteth of two Burgeffes out of every plantation wth out reftrainte or exception. Upon all thefe confiderations, the Affembly was contented to admitt of him and his Lieutenant (as members of their body and Burgeffes) into their society. Provided, that the faid Captaine Warde, wth all expedition, that is to faye between this and the nexte general affembly (all lawful impediments excepted), fhould procure from the Trefurer,[13] Counfell and Company in England a comiffion lawfully to eftablifh[14] and plant himfelfe and his Company as the Chieffs[15] of other Plantations have done. And in cafe he doe neglect this he is to ftande to the cenfure of the nexte generall affembly. To this Captaine Warde, in the prefence of us all, having given his confente and undertaken to perforne the fame, was, together wth his Lieutenant, by voices of the whole Affembly firft admitted to take the oath of Supremacy, and then to make up their number and to fitt amongft them.

This being done, the Governour himfelfe alledged that before we proceeded any further it behooved us to examine whither it were fitt, that Captaine Martin's Burgeffes fhoulde[16] have any place in the Affembly, forasmuche as he hath a claufe in his Patente wch doth not onely exempte him from that equality and uniformity of lawes and

---

[9] entered, McDonald. [10] soe, McDonald. [11] 30, Bancroft. [12] goode, McDonald. [13] Treasurer, McDonald. [14] establishe, McDonald, Bancroft. [15] Chiefes, McDonald. [16] should, Bancroft.

orders w[er][17] the great charter faith are to extende[18] over the whole Colony, but alfo from diverfe fuch lawes as we muft be enforced[19] to make in the General Affembly. •That claufe is as followeth: Item. That it fhall and may be lawfull to and for the faid Captain John Martin, his heyers, executours and affignes to governe and comaunde all fuche[20] person or perfons as at this time he fhall carry over with him, or that fhalbe[21] fente him hereafter, free from any comaunde of the Colony, excepte it be in ayding and affifting the fame againft[22] any forren or domeftical enemy.

Upon the[23] motion of the Governour, difcuffed the fame time in the affembly, enfued this order following:

An order of the General Affembly touching a claufe in Captain[24] Martin's Patent at James Citty, July 30, 1619.

After all the Burgeffes had taken the oath of Supremacy and were admitted into the houfe, and all fett downe in their places, a Copie of Captain[24] Martin's Patent[25] was produced by the Govern[or][26] out of a Claufe whereof it appeared that when the general[27] affembly had made fome kinde of lawes requifite for the whole Colony, he and his Burgeffes and people might deride the whole company and chufe whether they would obay[28] the fame or no.* It was therefore ordered in Courte that the forefaid two Burgeffes fhould wth drawe themfelves out of the affembly till fuche time as Captaine Martin had made his perfonall appearance before them. At what time, if upon their motion, if he would be contente to quitte and give over that parte of his Patente, and contrary therunto woulde submitte himfelfe to the general forme of governemente as all others did, that then his Burgeffes should be readmitted, otherwife they were utterly to be excluded as being fpies rather than[34] loyal Burgeffes, becaufe they had offered themfelves to be affistant at the making of [35] lawes w[ch] both themfelves and thofe whom they reprefented might chufe whether they would obaye[36] or not.

Then came there in a complainte againft Captain[37] Martin, that having fente his Shallop to trade for corne into the baye, under the commaunde of one Enfigne Harrifon, the faide Enfigne fhould affirme to one Thomas Davis, of Pafpaheighe,[38] Gent. (as the faid Thomas Davis depofed upon oathe,) that they had made a harde voiage, had

*The following passage is a side note on the margin of the McDonald and De Jarnette copies, but Bancroft includes it in the text:—The authority of Captaine[29] Martin's Patent graunted by the Counfell & Company under their Comon[30] Seale, being of an higher condition[31] and of greater[32] force then any Acte of the General[33] Affembly.

[17] W[ch], McDonald and Bancroft.   [18] extend, Bancroft.   [19] inforced, McDonald.   [20] such, McDonald. [21] shall be, McDonald.   [22] ag[st], McDonald.   [23] this, McDonald and Bancroft.   [24] Captaine, McDonald. [25] Patente, McDonald and Bancroft.   [26] Governour, McDonald and Bancroft.   [27] Generall, McDonald and Bancroft.   [28] obey, McDonald; obaye, Bancroft.   [29] Capt., McDonald.   [30] Common, McDonald.   [31] comission, McDonald.   [32] greater, McDonald.   [33] Generall.   [34] then, McDonald.   [35] of the, McD.   [36] obeye, McDonald; obaye, Bancroft.   [37] Captaine, McDonald and Bancroft.   [38] Paspaheighs, McDonald, Banc'ft.

they not mett wth a Canoa coming out of a creeke where their fhallop could not goe. For the Indians refufing to fell their Corne, thofe of the fhallop entered the Canoa wth their armes and tooke it by force, meafuring out the corne wth a bafkett they had into the Shallop and (as the faid Enfigne Harrifon faith) giving them fatisfaction in copper beades[39] and other trucking ftuffe.

Hitherto Mr. Davys upon his oath.

Furthermore it was fignified from Opochancano to the Governour that thofe people had complained to him to procure them juftice.[40] For wch confiderations and becaufe fuche[41] outrages as this might breede danger and loff[42] of life to others of the Colony wch fhould have leave to trade in the baye hereafter, and for prevention of the like violences againft the Indians in time to come, this order following was agreed on by the general affembly:

A fecond order againft Captain Martin, at James citty, July 30, 1619.

It was alfo ordered by the Affembly the fame daye that in cafe Captaine Martin and the ging of his fhallop would[43] not throughly anfwere an accufation of an outrage comitted againft a certaine Canoa of Indians in the baye, that then it was thought reafon (his Patent,[44] notw^{th}ftanding the authority whereof, he had in that cafe abufed) he fhoulde[45] from henceforth take leave of the Governour[46] as other men, and fhould putt[47] in fecurity, that his people fhall comitte no fuch[48] outrage any more.

Upon this a letter or warrant was drawen in the name of the whole affembly to fumon Captaine Martin to appeare before them in forme following:

By the Governo[49] and general affembly of Virginia.

Captaine Martine, we are to requeft[50] you upon fight hereof, with all convenient fpeed to repaire hither to James citty to treatt and conferre wth us about fome matters of efpeciall[51] importance, wch concerns[52] both us and the whole Colony and yourfelf. And of this we praye you not to faile.

James citty, July 30, 1619.

To our very loving friend, Captain John Martin, Efquire, Mafter of the ordinance.

Thefe obftacles removed, the Speaker, who a long time had bene

---

[39] beads, McDonald. [40] iuftice, McDonald. [41] such, McDonald. [42] loffe, McDonald. [43] could, McDonald, Bancroft. [44] Patente, McDonald and Bancroft. [45] should, Bancroft. [46] Governor. McDonald. [47] put, McDonald. [48] suche, McDonald and Bancroft. [49] Governour, Bancroft. [50] request, McDowell. [51] especiall, McDonald. [52] concerne, McDonald and Bancroft.

extreame fickly, and therefore not able to paffe through long har-
angues, delivered in briefe to the whole affembly the occafions of their
meeting. Which[53] done, he read unto them the comiffion for eftablifhing the Counfell of Eftate and the general[54] Affembly, wherein
their duties were defcribed to the life.

Having thus prepared them, he read over unto them the greate
Charter, or comiffion of priviledges, orders and lawes, sent by Sir
George Yeardley out of Englande.[55] Which[56] for the more eafe of the
Committies, having divided into fower books, he read the former two
the fame forenoon for expeditious[57] fake, a fecond time over, and fo
they were referred to the perufall of twoe Comitties, w[ch] did reciprocally
confider of either, and accordingly brought in their opinions. But
fome man may here objecte to what ende we fhould prefume to referre
that to the examination of Comitties w[ch] the Counfell and Company in
England[58] had already refolved to be perfect, and did expecte nothing[59] but our affente thereunto?[60] To this we anfwere, that we did it
not to the ende to correcte or controll anything therein contained, but
onely in cafe we fhould finde ought not perfectly fquaring wth the
ftate of this Colony or any lawe w[ch] did preffe or binde too harde, that
we might by waye of humble petition, feeke to have it redreffed, efpecially becaufe this great Charter is to binde us and our heyers for ever.

The names of the Comitties for perufing
the first booke of the fower:

1. Captain William Powell,	2. Enfigne Rofingham,
3. Captaine Warde,	4. Captaine Tucker,
5. Mr. Shelley,	6. Thomas Doufe,
7. Samuel Jordan,	8. Mr. Boys.

The names of the Comitties for perufing
the fecond booke:

1. Captaine Dawne,*	2. Captaine Graves,
3. Enfigne Spense,	4. Samuel Sharpe,
5. William Cap,	6. Mr. Pawlett,
7. Mr. Jefferfon,	8. Mr. Jackfon.

Thefe Comitties thus appointed, we brake up the firft forenoon's
affembly.

After dinner the Governo[r] and thofe that were not of the Comitties[61] fate a feconde time, while the faid Comitties[61] were employed in

---

[53]W[ch], McDonald. [54]Gen[ll], McDonald. [55]The substance of these will be found in the paper, "A
briefe Declaration," &c. See post. —. [56]W[ch], McDonald. [57]expeditions, Bancroft. [58]Englande, Mc-
Donald. [59]nothinge, McDonald. [60]thereunto, McDonald and Bancroft. [61]Comittees, McDonald.

*Lawne, McDonald, and Bancroft the list of Burgeffes on p. 10, showing this to be proper.

the perusall of thofe twoe bookes. And whereas the Speaker had propounded fower feverall objects for the Affembly to confider on: namely, firft, the great charter of orders, lawes and priviledges; Secondly, which of the inftructions given by the Counfel in England to my lo: la: warre,[62] Captain Argall or Sir George Yeardley, might conveniently putt on the habite of lawes; Thirdly, what lawes might iffue out of the private conceipte of any of the Burgeffes, or any other of the Colony; and laftly, what petitions were[63] fitt to be fente home for England. It pleafed the Governour[64] for expedition[65] fake to have the second objecte[66] of the fower to be examined & prepared by himfelfe and the Non-Comitties. Wherin after having fpente fome three howers'[67] conference, the twoe Committies[68] brought in their opinions concerning the twoe former bookes, (the fecond of which beginneth at thefe wordes of the Charter: And forafmuche as our intente is to eftablifh one equall and uniforme kinde of government over all Virginia &c.,)[69] w[ch] the whole Affembly, becaufe it was late, deferred to treatt[70] of till the next morning.

SATTURDAY, July 31.

The nexte daye, therefore, out of the opinions of the faid Comitties,[71] it was agreed, thefe[72] Petitions enfuing fhould be framed, to be prefented to the Treafurer, Counfel & Company in England. Upon the Comitties'[73] perufall of the firft booke,[74] the General[75] Affembly doe become moft humble fuitours to their lo[ps] and to the reft of that hon[ble] Counfell and renowned Company, that albeit they have bene pleafed[76] to allotte unto the Governo[r][77] to themfelves, together w[th] the Counfell of Eftate here, and[78] to the officers of Incorporations, certain lande[79] portions of lande to be layde out w[th]in the limites of the fame, yet that[80] they woulde vouchfafe alfo,[81] that[82] groundes as heretofore had bene granted by patent to the antient[83] Planters by former Governours that had from the Company received comiffion[84] fo to doe, might not nowe after so muche labour and cofte, and fo many yeares habitation be taken from them. And to the ende that no man might doe or fuffer any wrong in this kinde, that they woulde favour us fo muche (if they meane to graunte this our petition) as to fende us notice, what comiffion or authority for graunting of landes they have given to eache[85] particular Governour in times paste.

The fecond petition of the General affembly framed by the Co-

---

[62]Lord le Warre, McDonald. [63]we, McDonald. [64]Governor, McDonald. [65]expeditions, McDonald, also Bancroft. [66]obiecte, McDonald. [67]houres, McDonald. [68]two Comittees, McDonald. [69]The McDonald copy includes in ( ) all of this from "the second of which" to "Charter," and another single) after &c. The De Jarnette copy has one) only after &c. Bancroft includes what is adopted in this text. [70]McDonald has breath. [71]Comittees, McDonald. [72]those, McDonald. [73]Comittees, McDonald. [74]book, McDonald. [75]Generall, McDonald, [76]pleas'd, McDonald. [77]Govern[r] , McDonald; Gov[r] , Bancroft. [78]&, McDonald. [79]large, McDonald. [80]Bancroft omits "that." [81]alsoe, Bancroft. [82]McDonald has such and Bancroft suche after that, [83]ancient, McDonald. [84]Comiss[n] , Bancroft. [85]each, Bancroft.

mitties[86] out of the fecond book is. That the Treafurer[87] & Company
in England would be pleafed wth as muche convenient fpeed[88] as may
be to fende men hither to occupie their landes belonging to the fower
Incorporations, as well for their owne[89] behoofe and proffitt as for the
maintenance of the Counfel[90] of Eftate, who are nowe[91] to their extream hindrance often drawen far from their private bufines and likewife that they will have a care to fende[92] tenants to the minifters of the
fower Incorporations to manure their gleab, to the intente that the allowance they have allotted them of 200 G.[93] a yeare may the more
eafily be raifed.

The thirde Petition humbly prefented by this General Affembly to
the Treafurer, Counfell & Company is, that it may plainely be expreffed
in the great Comiffion (as indeed it is not) that the antient Planters of
both fortes, viz., fuche as before Sir Thomas Dales' depart[94] were come
hither upon their owne chardges,[95] and fuche also as were brought
hither upon the Companie's cofte, maye have their fecond, third and
more divifions fucceffively in as lardge and free manner as any other
Planters. Alfo that they wilbe pleafed to allowe to the male children,
of them and of all others begotten in Virginia, being the onely hope of
a pofterity, a fingle fhare a piece, and fhares for their iffues or[96] for
themfelves, becaufe that in a newe plantation it is not knowen whether
man or woman be the more neceffary.

Their fourth Petition is to befeech the Treafurer, Counfell & Company that they would be pleafed to appoint a Sub-Trefurer[97] here to
collecte their rents,[98] to the ende that[99] the Inhabitants of this Colony
be not tyed to an impoffibility of paying the fame yearly to the Treafurer in England, and that they would enjoine the faid Sub-Treafurer
not precifely according to the letter of the Charter to exacte mony of
us (whereof we have none at all, as we have no minte), but the true
value of the rente in comodity.

The fifte Petition is to befeeche the Treafurer, Counsell & Company that, towards the erecting of the Univerfity and Colledge, they
will fende, when they fhall thinke[100] it moft convenient, workmen of all
fortes, fitt for that purpofe.

The sixte and laste is, they wilbe[101] pleased to change the favage
name of Kiccowtan, and to give that Incorporation a newe name.

Thefe are the general Petitions drawen by the Comitties out of
the two former bookes w[ch] the whole general affembly in maner and
forme above[102] fett downe doe moft humbly offer up and prefent[103] to
the honourable conftruction of the Treafurer, Counfell and Company
in England.

---

[86]Comittess, McDonald.   [87]Tresurer, McDonald.   [88]speede, McDonald.   [89]own, Bancroft.   [90]Coun-
sell, McDonald and Bancroft.   [91]now, McDonald.   [92]send, McDonald.   [93]£200, Bancroft.   [94]In the Mc-
Donald copy this was just written departure, then "ure" croffed out with a pen, and the word made department.   Bancroft has departure.   [95]Charges, McDonald.   [96]McDonald and Bancroft both have "wives
as," instead of "iffues or," the former being evidently the proper words.   [97]Treasurer, McDonald.   [98]rentes,
McDonald, Bancroft.   [99]McDonald and Bancroft both omit that.   [100]McDonald and Bancroft omit it.
[101]will be, McDonald.   [102]sette, Bancroft.   [103]presente, McDonald and Bancroft.

Theſe petitions thus concluded on, thoſe twoe Comitties broughte me[104] a reporte what they had observed in the two latter bookes, wch was nothing elſe but that the perfection of them was ſuche as that [105] they could finde nothing therein ſubject to exception, only the Governors [106] particular opinion to my ſelfe in private hathe bene as touching a clauſe in the thirde booke, that in theſe doubtfull times between us and the Indians, it would beehoove[107] us not to make as[108] lardge distances between Plantation and Plantation as ten miles, but for our more ſtrength ande ſecurity to drawe nearer together.

At the ſame time, there remaining no[109] farther ſcruple in the mindes of the Aſſembly touching the ſaid great Charter of lawes, orders and priviledges, the Speaker putt the ſame to the queſtion, and ſo it had both the general aſſent and the applauſe of the whole aſſembly, who, as they profeſſed themſelves in the firſt place moſt ſubmiſſively thankfull to almighty god, therefore ſo they commaunded the Speaker to returne (as nowe he doth) their due and humble thankes to the Treasurer, Counſell and company for ſo many priviledges and favours as well in their owne names as in the names of the whole Colony whom they repreſented.

This being diſpatched we fell once more[110] debating of ſuche inſtructions given by the Counſell in England to ſeveral[111] Governors [112] as might be converted into lawes, the laſt whereof was the Eſtabliſhment of the price of Tobacco, namely, of the beſt at 3d[113] and the ſecond at 18d the pounde. At the reading of this the Aſſembly thought good to ſend for Mr. Abraham Perſey, the Cape marchant, to publiſhe this inſtruction to him, and to demaunde[114] of him if he knewe of any impediment why it might not be admitted of? His anſwere[115] was that he had not as yet received any ſuche order from the Adventurers of the[116] in England. And notwth ſtanding he ſawe the authority was good, yet was he unwilling to yield, till ſuche time as the Governor [117] and Aſſembly had layd their commandment upon him, out of the authority of the foreſaid Inſtructions as followeth:

By the General Aſſembly.

We will and require you, Mr. Abraham Perſey, Cape Marchant, from this daye forwarde to take notice, that, according to an article in the Inſtructions confirmed by the Treaſurer, Counſell[118] and Company in Englande at a general quarter courte, both by[119] voices and under their hands[120] and the Comon ſeall,[121] and given to Sir George Yeardley,

[104]In, McDonald, Bancroft. [105]McDonald and Bancroft omit that. [106]Govnrs, McDonald; Govrs, Bancroft. [107]Behoove, McDonald, Bancroft. [108]So, McDonald, Bancroft. [109]Noe, McDonald. [110]McDonald and Bancroft insert to. [111]Severall, McDonald. [112]Governrs, McDonald; Gov., Bancroft. [113]The text, which follows the De Jarnette copy, is evidently wrong. The McDonald copy is blotted and illegible. Bancroft has 3.s. and Sainsbury's abstract the same. [114]Demand, McDonald. [115]Answer, McDonald, Bancroft. [116]McDonald and Bancroft both fill the space with Magazin. [117]Govr, McDonald, Bancroft. [118]Counsell, Treasurer, McDonald. [119]McD. inserts the. [120]handes, McD. [121]seale, McD., Bft.

---

knight, this prefent governour, Decemb.[122] 3, 1618, that you are bounde to accepte of the Tobacco of the Colony, either for commodities or upon billes,[123] at three fhillings the befte[124] and the fecond forte at 18d the pounde, and this fhalbe[125] your fufficient difchardge.

James citty out of the faid General Affembly, July 31,[126] 1619.

At the fame[127] the Inftructions convertible into lawes were refer- red to the confideration of the above named Committies,[128] viz., the general Inftructions to the firft Committie[129] and the particular Inftruc- tions to the fecond, to be returned by them into the affembly on Mun- day morning.

SUNDAY, Aug. 1.

Mr. Shelley, one of the Burgeffes, deceased.

MUNDAY,[130] Aug. 2.

Captain John Martin (according to the fumons fent him on Fry- day,[131] July 30,) made his perfonall appearance at the barre, whenas the Speaker having firft read unto him the orders of the Affembly that concerned him, he pleaded lardgely for himfelf[132] to them both and in- devoured[133] to anfwere fome other thinges[134] that were objected againft[135] his Patente. In fine, being demanded out of the former or- der whether he would quitte that claufe of his Patent[136] w^{ch} (quite otherwife then Sir William Throckmorton's, Captain Chriftopher Dawnes'[137] and other men's patentes) exempteth himfelffe and his peo- ple from all fervices of the Colonie excepte onely in cafe of warre againft[138] a forren or domefticall enemie. His anfwere[139] was nega- tive, that he would not infringe any parte[140] of his Patente. Where- upon it was refolved by the Affembly that his Burgeffes fhould have no admittance.

To the fecond order his anfwere was affirmative, namely, that (his Patent[141] notwithftanding) whensoever he fhould fend into the baye to trade, he would[142] be contente to putt in fecurity to the Governour[143] for the good behaviour of his people towardes[144] the Indians.

It was at the fame time further ordered by the Affembly that the Speaker, in their names, fhould (as he nowe doth[145]) humbly de- maunde[146] of the Treafurer, Counfell[147] and Company an expofition of this one claufe in Captaine[148] Martin's Patente, namely, where it is faide That he is to enjoye[149] his landes in as lardge[150] and ample manner, to all

---

[122]Dec^r, McDonald. [123]bills, McDonald. [124]beft, McDonald. [125]fhall be, McDonald. [126]31st, Bancroft. [127]McDonald and Bancroft infert time. [128]Committees, McDonald. [129]Committee, McDonald. [130]Monday, McDonald and Bancroft. [131]Friday, McDonald. [132]himfelfe, McDonald and Bancroft. [133]& indeavoured, McDonald. [134]things, McDonald. [135]agst, McDonald. [136]Patente, McDonald and Bancroft. [137]Lawnes, Bancroft, fee p. 10. [138]agst, McDonald. [139]anfwer, Bancroft. [140]part, McDonald and Bancroft. [141]patente, McDonald. [142]woulde, McDonald. [143]Govr, Bancroft. [144]towards, Ban- croft. [145]doe, McDonald. [146]demande, McDonald. [147]Council, McDonald. [148]Capt., Bancroft, [149]en- joy, McDonald and Bancroft. [150]large, McDonald, Bancroft,

intentes and[151] purpofes, as any lord of any manours in England dothe holde his grounde out of w[ch] some have collected that he might by the fame graunte protecte men from paying their debts and from diverfe other dangers of lawe. The leaft the Affembly can alledge againft this claufe is, that it is obfcure, and that it is a thing impoffible for us here to knowe the Prerogatives of all the manours in Englande. The Affembly therefore humbly befeeche[152] their lo[pps] [153] and the reft of that hon[ble] houfe[154] that in cafe they fhall finde any thing in this or in any other parte of his graunte wherby that claufe towardes the conclu-fion of the great charter, (viz., that all grauntes afwell of the one forte as of the other refpectively, be made wth equall favour, & graunts[155] of like liberties & imunities[156] as neer as may be, to the ende that all com-plainte[157] of partiality and indifferency[158] may be avoided,) might [159] in any forte be contradicted or the uniformity and equality[160] of lawes and[161] orders extending over the whole Colony might be impeached, That they would be pleafed to remove any fuch hindrance as may di-verte out of the true courfe the free and[162] publique current of Juftice.

Upon the fame grounde and[163] reason their l[ops,] together with the reft of the Counfell[164] and Company, are humbly befought[165] by this general[166] affembly that if in that other claufe w[ch] exempteth Cap-taine[167] Martin and his people from all fervices of the Colony &c., they fhall finde any refiftance againft[168] that equality and[169] uniformity of lawes and orders intended nowe by them to be eftablifhed over the whole Colony, that they would be pleafed to reforme it.

In fine, wheras[170] Captaine[171] Martin, for thofe ten fhares allowed him for his perfonal[172] adventure and[173] for his adventure of £70 be-fides, doth claim 500 acres a fhare, that the Treafurer, Counfell and Company woulde vouchfafe to give notice to the Governour[174] here, what kinde[175] of fhares they meante he fhould have when they gave him his Patent.[176]

The premiffes about Captaine Martin thus refolved, the Commit-ties[177] appointed to confider what instructions are fitt to be converted into lawes, brought in their opinions, and[178] firft of fome of the gene-ral[179] inftructions.

> Here begin the lawes drawn out of the In-ftructions given by his Mat[ies] Counfell of Virginia in England to my lo: la warre,[180] Captain Argall and Sir George Yeardley, knight.

---

[151]&, McDonald. [152]befeecheth, McDonald and Bancroft. [153]Lop[s] , McDonald; L[ops], Bancroft. [154]bourde, McDonald and Bancroft. [155]grants, McDonald. [156]immunities, McDonald. [157]complaintes, McDonald, Bancroft. [158]unindifferency, McDonald, Bancroft. [159]mighte, McDonald. [160]equallity, Mc-Donald. [161]&, McDonald. [162]&, McDonald and Bancroft. [163]&, McDonald. [164]Councill, McDonald. [165]befoughte, McDonald. [166]the General, McDonald. [167]Captain, Bancroft. [168]ag[st], McDonald. [169]&, McDonald. [170]whereas, McDonald. [171]Captaine, McDonald; Capt., Bancroft. [172]perfonall, McDonald. [173]&, McDonald. [174]Govern[r] , McDonald. [175]kind, McDonald. [176]Patente, McDonald. [177]Comittee, McDonald. [178]&, McDonald. [179]generall, McDonald. [180]Lo. La Warre, McDonald and Bancroft.

By this prefent Generall Affembly be it enacted, that no[181] injury or oppreffion be wrought by the Englifhe[182] againft[183] the Indians whereby the prefent peace might be difturbed and antient quarrells might be revived.   And farther[184] be it ordained, that the Chicohomini are not to be excepted out of this lawe; untill either that suche [185] order come out of Englande, or that they doe provoke us by some newe injury.

Against Idlenes, Gaming, durunkenes & exceffe in apparell the Affembly hath enacted as followeth:

First, in deteftation of Idlenes[186] be it enacted, that if any men be founde to live as an Idler or renagate, though a freedman, it fhalbe [187] lawfull for that Incorporation or Plantation to wch he belongeth to ap-point him a Mr to ferve for wages, till he shewe apparant signes of amendment.

Againft gaming at dice[188] & Cardes be it ordained by this prefent affembly that the winner or winners fhall lofe all his or their winninges and[189] both winners and loofers fhall forfaicte[190] ten fhillings a man, one ten fhillings whereof to go to the difcoverer, and the reft to charitable & pious ufes in the Incorporation where the faulte[191] is comitted.

Againft drunkennefs be it alfo decreed that if any private perfon be found culpable thereof, for the firft time he is to be reprooved pri-vately by the Minifter, the fecond time publiquely, the thirde time to lye in boltes 12 howers in the houfe of the Provost Marfhall & to paye his fee,[192] and if he ftill continue in that vice, to undergo fuche fevere punifhment as the Governor[193] and Counfell of Eftate fhall thinke fitt to be inflicted on him.   But if any officer offende in this crime, the firft time he fhall receive a reprooff from the Governour, the fecond time he fhall openly be reprooved in the churche by the minifter, and the third time he fhall firft be comitted and then degraded.   Provided it be underftood that the Governr[194] hath alwayes[195] power to reftore him when he shall, in his difcretion thinke fitte.

Againft excesse in[196] apparell that every man be ceffed in the churche for all publique contributions, if he be unmarried according to his owne apparell, if he be married, according to his·owne and his wives, or either of their apparell.

As touching the inftruction[197] of drawing fome of the better dif-pofed of the Indians to converfe wth our people & to live and labour amongst[198] them, the Affembly who knowe[199] well their difpofitions thinke it fitte to enjoine,[200] leaft to counfell thofe of the Colony, neither utterly to rejecte them nor yet to drawe them to come in.   But in cafe

---

[181]Noe, McDonald.   [182]Englifhe, Bancroft.   [183]agst, McDonald.   [184]further, McDonald.   [185]fuch, McDonald.   [186]Idlers, McDonald.   [187]fhall be, McDonald.   [188]and, Bancroft.   [189]As the McDonald copy has & in every inftance where the other two have and, the reader will bear this in mind and it will not be again repeated.   [190]forfaite, McDonald.   [191]faults are, McDonald.   [192]fees, McDonald.   [193]Gov-ernr, McDonald; Governr , Bancroft.   [194]Governr, McDonald; Governr , Bancroft.   [195]alwaies, Mc-Donald; always, Bancroft.   [196]of, McDonald.   [197]inftructions, McDonald and Bancroft.   [198]among, Mc-Donald.   [199]know, McDonald.   [200]at inferted by Bancroft.

they will of themfelves come voluntarily to places well peopled, there to doe fervice in killing of Deere, fifhing, beatting of Corne and other workes, that then five or fix may be admitted into every fuch place, and no more, and that wth the confente[201] of the Governour. Provided that good[202] guarde[203] in the night be kept upon them, for generally (though fome amongft many may proove[204] good) they are a moft trecherous people and quickly gone when they have done a villany. And it were fitt[205] a houfewe builte for them to lodge in aparte[206] by themfelves, and lone inhabitants by no meanes[207] to entertaine them.

Be it enaćted by this prefent affembly that for laying a furer foundation of the converfion of the Indians to Chriftian Religion, eache towne, citty, Borrough, and particular plantation do obtaine unto themfelves by juft means a certaine number of the natives' children to be educated by them in true religion and civile courfe of life—of w[ch] children the moft towardly boyes in witt & graces of nature to be brought up by them in the firft elements of litterature, fo[208] to be fitted for the Colledge intended for them that from thence they may be fente[209] to that worke of converfion.

As touching the bufines of planting corne this prefent Affembly doth ordaine that yeare by yeare all & every houfeholder and houfe-holders have in ftore for every fervant he or they fhall keep, and alfo for his or their owne perfons, whether they have any Servants or no, one fpare barrell of corne, to be delivered out yearly, either upon fale or exchange as need fhall require. For the neglecte[210] of w[ch] duty he fhalbe[211] fubjecte to the cenfure of the Govern[r212] and Counfell of Eftate. Provided alwayes that the firft yeare of every newe man this lawe fhall not be of[213] force.

About the plantation of Mulbery trees, be it enaćted that every man as he is featted[214] upon his divifion, doe for feven yeares together, every yeare plante and maintaine in growte[215] fix[216] Mulberry trees at the leaft,[217] and as many more as he fhall thinke conveniente and as his virtue[218] & Induftry fhall move him to plante, and that all fuche perfons as fhall neglecte the yearly planting and maintaining of that fmall proportion fhalbe[219] fubjecte to the cenfure of the Governour & the Counfell of Eftate.

Be it farther[220] enaćted as concerning Silke-flaxe, that thofe men that are upon their divifion or fetled[221] habitation doe this next [222] yeare plante & dreffe 100 plantes, w[ch] being founde a comedity, [223] may farther be increafed. And whofoever do faill in the performance of this fhalbe[224] fubject to this punifhment of the Governour[225] & Counfell of Eftate.

---

[201]with confente, McDonald. [202]goode, Bancroft. [203]guard, McDonald. [204]prove, McDonald. [205]fitte, Bancroft. [206]apart, McDonald. [207]means, Bancroft. [208]as, inferted by Bancroft. [209]fent, McDonald. [210]neglect, McDonald. [211]fhall be, McDonald. [212]Governour, McDonald and Bancroft. [213]in, McDonald. [214]feated, McDonald. [215]growth, McDonald. [216]fixe, McDonald and Bancroft. [217]leafte, McDonald and Bancroft. [218]vertue, McDonald. [219]fhall be, McDonald. [220]further, McDonald. [221]fettled, McDonald. [222] next, McDonald. [223]comodity, McDonald and Bancroft. [224]fhall be, McDonald. [225]Governor, McDonald.

For hempe also both Englifhe & Indian, and for Englifhe[226] flax & Annifeeds, we do[227] require and enjoine all houfeholders of this Colony that have any of those seeds[228] to make tryal thereofe the nexte feason.

Moreover be it enacted by this present Affembly, that every houfeholder doe yearly plante and maintaine ten vines untill they have attained to the art and experience of dressing a Vineyard either by their owne induftry or by the Instruction of fome Vigneron. And that upon what penalty foever the Governo[r][229] and Counfell of Eftate fhall thinke fitt to impofe upon the neglecters of this acte.

Be it alfo enacted that all neceffary tradefmen, or fo[230] many as need fhall require, suche[231] as are come over fince the departure of Sir Thomas Dale, or that fhall hereafter come, fhall worke at their trades for any other man, each[232] one being payde according to the quality [233] of his trade and worke, to be eftimated, if he fhall not be contented, by the Governo[r] and officers of the place where he worketh.

Be it further ordained by this General Affembly, and we doe by thefe prefents enacte, that all contractes[234] made in England between the owners of lande and their Tenants and Servantes w[ch] they fhall fende[235] hither, may be caufed to be duely[236] performed, and that the offenders be punifhed as the Governour[237] and Counfell of Eftate fhall thinke just and convenient.

Be it eftablifhed alfo by this prefent Affembly that no crafty or advantagious means be fuffered to be putt in practife for the inticing awaye the Tenants or[238] Servants of any particular plantation from the place where they are seatted. And that it fhalbe[239] the duty of the Governo[r][240] & Counfell of Eftate moft feverely to punifhe both the feducers and the feduced, and to returne[241] thefe latter into their former places.

Be it further enacted that the orders for the Magazin[242] lately made be exactly kepte, and that the Magazin be preferved from wrong[243] and finifter practifes, and that according to the orders of courte in Englande[244] all Tobacco and faffafras be brought[245] by the Planters to the Cape marchant till fuche time as all the goods[246] nowe or heretofore fent for the Magazin be taken off their handes at the prices agreed on. That by this meanes[247] the fome[248] going for Englande[249] with[250] one hande, the price thereof may be uphelde[251] the better. And to the ende that all the whole Colony may take notice of the laft order of Courte made in Englande and all thofe whom it concerneth may knowe[252] howe[253] to obferve it, we[254] holde it fitt to publifhe it

[226]Englifh, Bancroft. [227]wee doe, McDonald. [228]feedes, Bancroft. [229]Governour, McDonald and Bancroft. [230]foe, McDonald. [231]fuch, Bancroft. [232]eache, McDonald and Bancroft. [233]qualitye, Bancroft. [234]contracts, McDonald. [235]fend, McDonald. [236]duly, McDonald. [237]Gover[nr], McDonald. [238]&, McDonald. [239]fhall be, McDonald. [240]Gover[nr], McDonald; Governour, Bancroft. [241]return, Bancroft. [242]magazine, McDonald. [243]wronge, McDonald. [244]England, McDonald. [245]Sasfafras brought, McDonald; to be brought, Bancroft. [246]goodes, Bancroft. [247]means, Bancroft. [248]fame, McDonald and Bancroft. [249]England, McDonald. [250]into, McDonald and Bancroft. [251]upheld, Bancroft. [252]know, McDonald. [253]how, McDonald. [254]wee, McDonald.

here for a lawe[255] among the reft of our lawes. The w[ch] [256] order is as followeth:

Upon the 26[257] of October, 1618, it was ordered that the Maga-zin[258] fhould continue during[259] the terme formerly prefixed, and that certaine[260] abufes now complained of fhould be reformed, and that for preventing of all Impofitions fave the allowance of 25 in the hundred proffitt, the Governo[r][261] fhall have an invoice as well as the Cape Mar-chant, that if any abuse in the fale of the[262] goods be offered, wee, [263] upon Intelligence and due examination thereof, fhall fee it correctede. And for the incouragement[264] of particular hundreds, as Smythe's hun-dred, Martin's hundred, Lawnes' hundred, and the like, it is agreed that what comodities are reaped upon anie of thefe General[265] Colonies, it fhalbe lawfull for them to returne the fame to their owne adventurers. Provided that the fame[266] comodity be of their owne growing, wth out trading wth any other, in one entyre lumpe and not difperfed, and that at the determination of the jointe ftocke, the goods then remaining in the Magazin[267] fhalbe[268] bought by the faid particular Colonies before any other goods w[ch] fhall be fente by private men. And it was more-over ordered that if the lady la warre, the Lady Dale, Captain Bar-grave and the reft, would unite themfelves into a fettled[269] Colony they might be capable of the same priviledges that are graunted to any of the forefaid hundreds. Hitherto the order.

All[270] the general Affembly by voices concluded not only the ac-ceptance and obfervation of this order, but of the Inftruction alfo to Sir George Yeardley next preceding the fame. Provided firft, that the Cape Marchant do[271] accepte of the Tobacco of all and everie the Planters here in Virginia, either for Goods or upon billes of Exchange at three fhillings the pounde the befte, and 18d the fecond sorte. Pro-vided alfo that the billes be only payde in Englande. Provided, in the third place, that if any other befides the Magazin[272] have at any time any neceffary comodity w[ch] the Magazine doth wante, it fhall and may be lawfull for any of the Colony to buye[273] the faid neceffary comodity of the faid party, but upon the termes of the Magazin[274] viz: allowing no more gaine then 25 in the hundred, and that with the leave of the Governour. Provided laftly,[275] that it may be lawfull[276] for the Gov-ern[r][277] to give leave to any Mariner, or any other perfon, that fhall have any fuche neceffary comodity wanting to the Magazin[278] to carrie home for England so muche[279] Tobacco or other naturall comodities of the Country[280] as his Customers fhall pay him for the faid neceffary comodity or comodities. And to the ende we may not only persuade

---

[255]Law, McDonald. [256]which, McDonald. [257]26th, McDonald and Bancroft. [258]Magazine, McDon-ald. [259]duringe, McDonald. [260]certain, Bancroft. [261]Governour, McDonald and Bancroft. [262]the, omitted by McDonald. [263]wee, McDonald, Bancroft. [264]encouragement, McDonald. [265]feverall, Mc-Donald; feveral, Bancroft; this word evidently the proper one. [266]faid, McDonald, Bancroft. [267]maga-zine, McDonald. [268]fhall be, McDonald. [269]fetled, Bancroft. [270]And, Bancroft. [271]doe, McDonald. [272]magazine, McDonald. [273]buy, McDonald. [274]magazine, McDonald. [275]lastly, McDonald. [276]lawful, McDonald. [277]Governour, McDonald and Bancroft. [278]As this word is fpelt by McDonald in every in-ftance with the final e this note will not be repeated. [279]much, McDonald. [280]countrey, McDonald.

and incite men, but inforce them alfo thoroughly and loyally to aire their Tobacco before they bring it to the Magazine,[281] be it enacted, and by these presents we doe enacte, that if upon the Judgement of power sufficient even of any incorporation where the Magazine[282] shall refide, (having first taken their oaths to give true fentence, twoe where-of to be chofen by the Cape Marchant and twoe by the Incorporation,) any Tobacco whatfoever fhall not proove[283] vendible at the fecond price, that it fhall there imediately be burnt before the owner's face. Hitherto fuche lawes as were drawen out of the Instructions.

TUESDAY, Aug. 3,[284] 1619.

This morning a thirde[285] forte of lawes (fuche as might proceed out of every man's private conceipt[286]) were read and referred by halves to the fame comitties[287] wch were from the beginning.

This done, Captaine[288] William Powell prefented to the Affembly a petition to have juftice againft a lewde[289] and trecherous servante of his who by falfe accufation given up in writing to the Governo^r [290] fought not onely to gett[291] him depofed from his government of James citty and utterly (according to the Proclamation) to be degraded from the place and title of a Captaine, but to take his life from him also. And fo out of the faid Petition fprang this order following:

Captaine William Powell prefented a Petition to the generall [292] Affembly againft[293] one Thomas Garnett, a servant of his, not onely for extreame neglect of his bufineff to the great loff [294] and prejudice of the faid Captaine, and for openly and impudently abufing his house, in fight both of Mafter and Miftreffe, through wantonnes[295] wth a woman fervant of theirs, a widdowe, but alfo for falsely accufing him to the Governo^r [296] both of Drunkenes &[297] Thefte, and befides for bringing all[298] his fellow fervants to teftifie[299] on his side, wherein they juftly failled[300] him. It was thought fitt by the general affembly (the Governour himfelfe[301] giving fentence), that he fhould ftand[302] fower dayes with his eares nayled to the Pillory, viz: Wednesday, Aug. 4th, and fo likewife Thurfday, fryday and Saturday[303] next following, and every of thofe fower dayes fhould be publiquely whipped. Now, as touching the neglecte of his worke, what fatisfaction ought to be made to his M^r for that is referred to the Governour and Counfell of Eftate.

The fame morning the lawes abovewritten, drawen out of the in-ftructions, were read, and one by one thoroughly examined, and then paffed once againe[304] the general[305] confente of the whole Affembly.

---

[281]Magazin, Bancroft. [282]do., do. [283]prove, Bancroft. [284]3rd, Bancroft. [285]third, Bancroft. [286]con-ceipte, McDonald and Bancroft. [287]comities, Bancroft. [288]Capt., Bancroft. [289]lewd, McDonald. [290]Gov-ernour, McDonald and Bancroft. [291]get, McDonald. [292]General, McDonald. [293]ag^st, McDonald. [294]loffe, McDonald and Bancroft.. [295]wantonnes, McDonald; wantonnefs, Bancroft. [296]Governour, McDonald and Bancroft. [297]McDonald omits the & ; Bancroft, nor and. [298]McDonald omits the all. [299]certifie, Ban-croft. [300]failed, McDonald, Bancroft. [301]himfelf, McDonald. [302]ftande, McDonald, Bancroft. [303]Satur-day, Bancroft. [304]againe, McDonald, Bancroft. [305]generall, McDonald, Bancroft.

This afternoon the committies brought in a reporte, what they had done as concerning the third forte of lawes, the difcuffing whereof fpente the refidue of that daye. Excepte onely the confideration of a petition of M[r] John Rolfes againfte Captaine John Martine[306] for writing a letter to him wherein (as M[r] Rolfe alledgeth) he taxeth him both unfeemly[307] and amiffe of certaine thinges[308] wherein he was never faulty, and befides, cafteth fome afperfion upon the prefent government, w[ch] is the moft temperate and jufte[309] that ever was in this country, too milde, indeed, for many of[310] this Colony, whom unwoonted[311] liberty hath made infolente and not to knowe[312] themfelves. This Petition of M[r] Rolfes' was thought fitt to be referred to the Counfell of State.

WEDENSDAY, Aug. 4th.

This daye (by reafon of extream heat, both pafte and likely to enfue, and by that meanes of the alteration of the healthes of diverfe of the general Affembly) the Governour, who[313] himfelfe alfo[314] was not well, refolved fhould be the laft of this firft feffion; fo in the morning the Speaker (as he was required by the Affembly) redd over all the lawes and orders that had formerly paffed the houfe, to give the fame yett one reviewe[315] more, and to fee whether there were any thing to be amended or that might be excepted againfte. This being done, the third forte of lawes w[ch] I am nowe coming[316] to fett downe, were read over throughly[317] difcuffed, w[ch], together wth the former, did now paffe the lafte and finall confente of the General[318] Affembly.

A third forte of lawes, fuche as may[319] iffue out of
every man's private[320] conceipte.

It fhalbe free for every man to trade wth the Indians, fervants onely excepted, upon paine of whipping, unlefs the M[r] will[321] redeeme it off wth the payment of an Angell, one-fourth parte whereofe to go[322] to the Provoft Marfhall, one fourth parte to the difcoverer, and the other moyty to the publique ufes of the Incorporation.[323]

That no man doe[324] fell or give any of the greater howes to the Indians, or any Englifhe dog of quality, as a maftive,[326] greyhound, bloodhounde, lande or water fpaniel, or any other dog or bitche whatfoever, of the Englifhe race, upon paine of forfaiting 5[s] [327] sterling to the publique ufes of the Incorporation where he dwelleth.

That no man do fell or give any Indians any piece fhott or poulder, or any other armes, offenfive or defenfive, upon paine of being held a

[306]Martin, McDonald. [307]unfeemingly, Bancroft. [308]things, McDonald, Bancroft. [309]juft, McDonald. [310]in, McDonald. [311]unwonted, McDonald. [312]know, McDonald. [313]who, omitted by McDonald. [314]who, inferted by McDonald. [315]review, McDonald. [316]cominge, McDonald. [317]thoroughly, McDonald. [318]generall, McDonald. [319]maye, Bancroft. [320]privat, McDonald, Bancroft. [321]will, omitted by McDonald. [322]goe, McDonald. [323]where he dwelleth, added in McDonald copy. [324]do, McDonald, Bancroft. [325]Englifh, McDonald. [326]maftiffe, McDonald. [227]5[b] , McDonald; £5, Bancroft.

4

Traytour to the Colony, and of being hanged as foon as the facte [328] is proved, w[th]out all redemption.[329]

That no man may go above twenty miles from his dwelling-place, nor upon any voiage whatfoever fhalbe abfent from thence for the fpace of feven dayes together w[th]out firft having made the Governo[r] [330] or comaunder of the fame place acquainted therw[th], [331] upon paine[332] of paying twenty fhillinges[333] to the publique ufes of the fame Incorporation where the party delinquent dwelleth.

That noe man fhall purpofely goe to any Indian townes, habitations or places of refort[334] w[th]out leave from the Governo[r] [335] or comaunder[336] of that place where he liveth, upon paine of paying 40[s] to publique ufes as aforefaid.

That no man living in this Colony, but fhall between this and the firft of January nexte enfuing come or fende to the Secretary of Eftate [337] to enter his own and all his fervants' names, and for what terme or upon what conditions they are to ferve, upon penalty of paying 40[s] to the faid Secretary of Eftate.[338] Alfo, whatfoever M[rs] or people doe[339] come over to this plantation that within[340] one month of their arrivall (notice being firft given them of this very lawe) they fhall likewife reforte to the Secretary of Eftate[341] and fhall certifie him upon what termes or conditions they be come hither, to the ende that he may recorde their grauntes and comiffions, and for how long time and upon what conditions[342] their fervants (in cafe they have any) are to ferve them, and that upon paine of the penalty nexte above mentioned.

All Minifters in the Colony fhall once a year, namely, in the moneth of Marche, bring to the Secretary of Eftate a true account of all Chriftenings, burials and marriages, upon paine, if they faill, to be cenfured for their negligence by the Governo[r] [343] and Counfell[344] of Eftate; likewife, where there be no minifters, that the comanders of the place doe fupply the fame duty.

No man, w[th]out leave of the Governo[r] , fhall kill any Neatt cattle whatfoever, young or olde, efpecially kine, Heyfurs or cow-calves, and fhalbe[345] carefull to preferve their fteeres[346] and oxen, and to bring them to the plough and fuch profitable ufes, and w[th]out having obtained leave as aforefaid, fhall not kill them, upon penalty of forfaiting the value of the beaft fo killed.

Whofoever fhall take any of his neighbours' boates, oares, or canoas w[th]out leave from the owner fhalbe held[348] and efteemed as a felon and fo proceeded againfte;[349] tho[350] hee that fhall take away by violence or ftelth any canoas or other thinges from the Indians fhall make

[328]Fact, McDonald. [329]In the McDonald copy this and the paragraph next preceding are transposed. [330]Governour, McDonald, Bancroft. [331]therewith, McDonald, Bancroft. [332]penalty, McDonald. [333]fhillings, Bancroft. [334]reforte, McDonald, Bancroft. [335]Gover[n]r , McDonald; Governour, Bancroft. [336]comander, McDonald; comand[r] , Bancroft. [337]State, McDonald. [338]State, McDonald. [339]do., Bancroft. [340]w[th]in, McDonald. [341]State, McDonald. [342]In the McDonald copy, from the word conditions, in the third line above, to this point are omitted. [343]Governour, McDonald, Bancroft. [344]Councill, McDonald. [345]fhall be, McDonald, Bancroft. [346]steers, McDonald. [348]helde, McDonald, Bancroft. [349]againft, McDonald, Bancroft. [350]alfo McDonald, Bancroft.

valuable reſtitution to the ſaid Indians, and ſhall forſaiƈt, if he be a free-holder, five pound; if a ſervant, 40ˢ , or endure a whipping; and any-thing under the value of 13ᵈ ³⁵¹ ſhall be accounted Petty larceny.

All miniſters ſhall duely read divine ſervice, and exercise their miniſterial funƈtion according to the Eccleſiaſtical lawes and orders of the churche³⁵² of Englande, and every Sunday in the afternoon³⁵³ ſhall Catechize ſuche as are not yet ripe to come to the Com.³⁵⁴ And who-ſoever of them ſhalbe³⁵⁵ found negligent or faulty in this kinde ſhalbe ſubjeƈt to the cenſure of the Governʳ and Counſell of Eſtate.

The Miniſters and Churchwardens ſhall ſeeke to preſente³⁵⁶ all un-godly diſorders, the comitters wherofe³⁵⁷ if, upon goode³⁵⁸ admonitions and milde reprooff,³⁵⁹ they will not forbeare the ſaid ſkandalous of-fenſes,³⁶⁰ as ſuſpicions of whordomes,³⁶¹ diſhoneſt company keeping with weomen and ſuche³⁶² like, they are to be preſented and puniſhed ac-cordingly.

If any perſon after two warnings, doe³⁶³ not amende³⁶⁴ his or her life in point³⁶⁵ of evident ſuſpicion of Incontincy³⁶⁶ or of the comiſſion³⁶⁷ of any other enormous ſinnes,³⁶⁸ that then he or ſhee be preſented by the Churchwardens and ſuſpended for a time from the churche by the miniſter. In wᶜʰ Interim if the ſame perſon do³⁶⁹ not amende and humbly ſubmit³⁷⁰ him or herſelfe to the churche, he is then fully to be excomunicate and ſoon after a writt or warrant to be ſent³⁷¹ from the Governʳ ³⁷² for the apprehending of his perſon ande ſeizing on³⁷³ all his goods. Provided alwayes, that all the miniſters doe meet³⁷⁴ once a quarter, namely, at the feaſt of Sᵗ Michael the Arkangell, of the na-tivity of our ſaviour, of the Annuntiation of the bleſſed Virgine, and about midſomer, at³⁷⁵ James citty or any other place where the Gov-ernoʳ ³⁷⁶ ſhall reſide, to determine whom it is fitt to excomunicate, and that they firſt preſente their opinion to the Governoʳ ³⁷⁷ ere they pro-ceed to the acte of excomunication.

For reformation of ſwearing, every freeman and Mʳ of a family after thriſe admonition ſhall give 5s or the value upon preſent³⁷⁸ de-maunde, to the uſe of the church where he dwelleth; and every ſervant after the like admonition, excepte his Mʳ diſchardge³⁷⁹ the fine, ſhalbe ſubjeƈt to whipping. Provided, that the payment of the fine notwᵗʰ-ſtanding, the ſaid ſervant ſhall acknowledge his faulte publiquely in the Churche.

No man whatſoever, coming by water from above, as from Hen-rico, Charles citty, or any place from the weſtwarde of James citty, and

---

³⁵¹13 ob., McDonald. ³⁵²Church, McDonald. ³⁵³afternoone, McDonald. ³⁵⁴comunion, McDonald, Bancroft. ³⁵⁵ſhall be, McDonald. ³⁵⁶prevente, McDonald, Bancroft. ³⁵⁷whereof, McDonald, Bancroft. ³⁵⁸good, McDonald, Bancroft. ³⁵⁹reproofe, McDonald. ³⁶⁰offences, McDonald. ³⁶¹whoredoms, McDonald. ³⁶²ſuch, McDonald. ³⁶³do., Bancroft. ³⁶⁴amend, Bancroft. ³⁶⁵pointe, McDonald. ³⁶⁶Incontinency, Mc-Donald, Bancroft. ³⁶⁷commiſſion, McDonald. ³⁶⁸ſuines, Bancroft. ³⁶⁹doe, McDonald. ³⁷⁰ſubmitt, Mc-Donald, Bancroft. ³⁷¹ſente, McDonald, Bancroft. ³⁷²Governour, Bancroft. ³⁷³McDonald omits on. ³⁷⁴meete, McDonald. ³⁷⁵att., McDonald. ³⁷⁶Goverⁿʳ, McDonald; Governour, Bancroft. ³⁷⁷Governour, McDonald, Bancroft. ³⁷⁸preſente, McDonald. ³⁷⁹diſcharge, McDonald.

being bound for Kiccowtan,[380] or any other parte on this fide,[381] the fame fhall prefume to pafs by, either by day or by night, w[th]out touching firfte here at James citty to knowe[382] whether the Governo[r][383] will comande him any fervice. And the like fhall they performe that come from Kicawtan[384] ward, or from any place between this and that, to go upwarde, upon paine of forfaiting ten pound fterling a time to the Govern[r][385]. Provided, that if a fervant having had inftructions from his Mafter to obferve this lawe,[386] doe, notw[th]ftanding, tranfgreffe the fame, that then the faid[387] fervant fhalbe punifhed at the Governr[r][s] difcretion; otherwife, that the mafter himfelfe fhall undergo the forefaid penalty.

No man fhall trade[388] into the baye, either in fhallop, pinnace, or fhip, w[th]out the Govern[r][s][389] licenfe, and w[th]out putting in fecurity that neither himfelf nor his Company fhall force or wrong the Indians, upon paine that, doing otherwife, they fhalbe cenfured at their returne by the Govern[or] [390] and Counfell[391] of Eftate.

All perfons whatfoever upon the Sabaoth daye[392] fhall frequente divine fervice and fermons both forenoon and afternoon, and all fuche as beare armes fhall bring[393] their pieces, fwordes, poulder and fhotte. And every one that fhall tranfgreffe this lawe fhall forfaicte[394] three fhillinges[395] a tim~ to the ufe of the churche, all lawful and neceffary impediments excepted. But if a fervant in this cafe fhall wilfully neglecte his M[r][s] comande he fhall fuffer bodily punifhmente.

No maide or woman fervant, either now refident in the Colonie or hereafter to come, fhall contract herfelfe in marriage w[th]out either the confente of her parents, or of her M[r] or M[ris], or of the magiftrat[396] and minifter of the place both together. And whatfoever minifter fhall marry or contracte any fuche perfons w[th]out fome of the forefaid confentes fhalbe[397] fubjecte to the fevere cenfure of the Govern[r] [398] and Counfell[399] of Eftate.

Be it enacted by this[400] prefent affembly that whatfoever fervant hath heretofore or fhall hereafter contracte himfelfe in England, either by way of Indenture or otherwife, to ferve any Mafter here in Virginia and fhall afterward, againft[401] his faid former contracte, depart from his M[r] w[th]out leave, or, being once imbarked, fhall abandon the fhip he is appointed to come in, and fo, being lefte behinde, fhall putt[402] himfelfe into the fervice of any other man that will bring him hither, that then at the fame fervant's arrival here, he fhall firft ferve out his time with that M[r] that brought him hither and afterward alfo fhall ferve out his time[403] wth his former M[r] according to his covenant.

Here ende the lawes.

---

[380]Kicowtan, Bancroft. [381]of, inferted by McDonald. [382]know, McDonald. [383]Governour, McDonald, Bancroft. [384]Kiccowtan, McDonald, Bancroft. [385]Governor, McDonald, Bancroft. [386]McDonald reads, obferve his fervice. [387]s[d], McDonald. [388]fhall have trade, Bancroft. [389]Governour's, McDonald, Bancroft. [390]Governour, McDonald; Gov[r], Bancroft. [391]Councell, McDonald. [392]days, McDonald, Bancroft. [393]bringe, McDonald. [394]forfaict, Bancroft. [395]fhillings, Bancroft. [396]magiftrate, McDonald, Bancroft. [397]fhall be, McDonald, Bancroft. [398]Gover[nr], McDonald; Gov[r], Bancroft. [399]Council, McDonald. [400]the, McDonald. [401]ag[st], McDonald. [402]put, McDonald, Bancroft. [403]McDonald omits the words, with that M[r] that brought him hither and afterwards alfo fhall ferve out his time.

All thefe lawes being thus concluded and confented to as afore-
faide[404] Captaine Henry Spellman[405] was called to the barre to anfwere
to certaine mifdemeano[rs] layde to his chardge by Robert Poole, inter-
pretour, upon his oath (whofe examination the Governo[r] fente into
England in the Profperus), of w[ch] accufations of Poole fome he ac-
knowledged for true, but the greatteft[406] part he denyed. Whereupon
the General[407] Affembly, having throughly heard and confidered his
fpeaches, did conftitute this order following againft him:

Aug. 4th, 1619.

This day Captaine Henry Spelman[408] was convented before the
General Affembly and was examined by a relation upon oath of one
Robert Poole, Interpreter, what conference had paffed between the
faid Spelman[409] and Opochancano at Poole's meeting with him in
Opochancano's courte. Poole chardgeth him he fpake very unrev-
erently and malicioufly againft[410] this prefent Govern[r] ,[411] wherby the
honour and dignity of his place and perfon, and fo of the whole Colonie,
might be brought into contempte, by w[ch] meanes what mifchiefs might
enfue from the Indians by difturbance of the peace or otherwife, may
eafily be conjectured. Some thinges of this relation Spelman confeffed,
but the moft parte he denyed, excepte onely one matter of importance,
& that was that he hade informed Opochancano that w[th]in a yeare
there would come a Governo[r] [412] greater then[413] this that nowe is in
place. By w[ch] and by other reportes it feemeth he hath alienated the
minde of Opochancano from this prefent Governour, and brought him
in much difefteem, both w[th] Opochancano[414] and the Indians, and the
whole Colony in danger of their flippery defignes.

The general affembly upon Poole's teftimony onely not willing to
putt Spelman to the rigour and extremity of the lawe, w[ch] might, perhaps both fpeedily and defervedly, have taken his life from him (upon
the witnefs[415] of one whom he muche excepted againft) were pleafed,
for the prefent, to cenfure him rather out of that his confeffion above
written then[416] out of any other prooffe. Several and fharpe punifhments were pronounced againft[417] him by diverfe of the Affembly, But
in fine the whole courfe[418] by voices united did encline to the moft fa-
vourable, w[ch] was that for this mifdemeanour[419] he fhould firft be degraded of his title of Captaine,[420] at the head of the troupe, and fhould
be condemned to performe feven yeares fervice to the Colony in the
nature of Interpreter to the Governour.

This fentence being read to Spelman he, as one that had in him
more of the Savage then of the Chriftian, muttered certaine wordes to

[404]Aforefaid, Bancroft. [405]Spelman, McDonald. [406]greateft, McDonald. [407]gen[l] , Bancroft. [408]Spell-
man, Bancroft. [409]Spellman, Bancroft. [410]ag[st] , McDonald. [411]Governour, Bancroft. [412]Governour,
McDonald, Bancroft. [413]than, McDonald, Bancroft. [414]Opochancanos, McDonald. [415]witnes, McDonald, Bancroft. [416]than, Bancroft. [417]ag[st] , McDonald. [418]courte, McDonald, Bancroft. [419]mifdemeanor,
McDonald; mifdemean[r] , Bancroft. [420]Capt., McDonald.

himfelfe neither fhewing any remorfe for his offences, nor yet any thankfulnefs to the Affembly for theire fofavourable cenfure, w[ch] he at one time or another (God's grace not wholly abandoning him) might wth fome one fervice have been able to have redeemed.*

This day alfo did the Inhabitants of Pafpaheigh, alias Argall's towne, prefent a petition to the general affembly to give them an abfolute difchardge from certaine bondes wherin they ftand bound to Captain Samuell Argall for the paym[t] of 600[G],[421] and to Captain William Powell, at Captaine Argall's appointment, for the paym[t] of 50[G] [422] more. To Captaine Argall for 15 fkore acres of wooddy ground, called by the name of Argal's[423] towne or Pafpaheigh; to Captaine Powell in refpect of his paines in clearing the grounde and building the houfes, for w[ch] Captaine[424] Argal ought to have given him fatisfaction. Nowe,[425] the general affembly being doubtful whether they have any power and authority to difchardge the faid bondes, doe by thefe prefents[426] (at the Inftance of the faid Inhabitants[427] of Pafpaheighs, alias Martin's hundred people) become moft humble futours to the Trefurer, Counfell and Company in England that they wilbe[428] pleafed to gett the faid bondes for 600[G] [429] to be cancelled; forasmuche as in their great comiffion they have expreffly and by name appointed that place of Pafpaheigh for parte of the Governor's[430] lande. And wheras Captain[431] William Powell is payde[432] his 50[G] w[ch] Captaine[433] Argall enjoined the faide Inhabitantes to prefente him with, as parte[434] of the bargaine, the general affembly, at their intreaty, do become futours on their behalfe, that Captaine Argall, by the Counfell & Company in England, may be compelled either to reftore the faid 50[G] [435] from thence, or elfe that reftitution therof be made here out of the goods of the faid Captaine Argall.

The laft acte of the Generall Affembly was a contribution to gratifie their officers, as followeth:†

AUG. 4th, 1619.

It is fully agreed at this generall[436] Affembly that in regarde of the great[437] paines and labour of the[438] Speaker of this Affembly (who not onely[439] firft formed the fame Affembly and to their great eafe & expedition reduced all matters to be treatted of into a ready method, but alfo his indifpofition notw[th]ftanding wrote or dictated all orders and other expedients and is yet[440] to write feverall bookes for all the Generall[441]

---

* This paragraph appears only in the McDonald copy, and in that it has two rows of lines at right angles to each other and diagonally across it, as if to indicate that this portion of the record was confidered as being improperly made or, perhaps, was not official.

† This paragraph is in the McDonald and Bancroft copies but not in De Jarnette's.

[421]600L[l], McDonald; £60, Bancroft. [422]50[ll], McDonald; £50, Bancroft. [423]Argall's, McDonald. [424]Capt., Bancroft. [425]now, McDonald. [426]prefentes, McDonald, Bancroft. [427]Inhabit[ts], Bancroft. [428]will be, McDonald, Bancroft. [429]600[ll], McDonald; £60, Bancroft. [430]Governours, McDonald, Bancroft. [431]Captaine, McDonald, Bancroft. [432]paide, Bancroft. [433]Capt., Bancroft. [434]part, Bancroft. [435]50[ll], McDonald; £50, Bancroft. [436]general, McDonald. [437]greate, Bancroft. [438]this, McDonald. [439]only, McDonald. [440]yett, Bancroft. [441]feverall, McDonald, Bancroft.

Incorporations and plantations both of the great charter, and of all the lawes) and likewife in refpecte of the dilligence of the Clerke and fergeant, officers thereto belonging. That every man and manfervant of above 16 yeares of age fhall pay into the handes and Cuftody of the Burgeffes of every Incorporation and plantation one pound of the beft Tobacco, to be diftributed to the Speaker and likewife to the Clerke and fargeant of the Affembly, according to their degrees and rankes, the whole bulke whereof to be delivered into the Speaker's handes, to be divided accordingly. And in regarde[442] the Provoft Marfhall of James citty hath alfo given fome attendance upon the faid Generall Affembly, he is alfo to have a fhare out of the fame. And this is to begin to be gathered the 24th of February nexte.

In conclufion, the whole Affembly comaunded[443] the Speaker (as nowe he doth) to prefent their humble excufe to the Treafurer[444] Counfell & Company in England for being conftrained by the intemperature of the weather and the failing fick of diverfe of the Burgeffes to breake up fo abruptly—before they had fo much as putt their lawes to the ingroffing. This they wholly comited to[445] the fidelity of their fpeaker, who therin[446] (his confcience telles him) hath done the parte[447] of an honeft man, otherwife he would be eafily founde[448] out by the Burgeffes themfelves, who wth all expedition are to have fo many bookes of the fame lawes as there be both Incorporations and Plantations in the Colony.

In the feconde place, the Affembly doth moft humbly crave pardon that in fo fhorte[449] a fpace they could bring their matter to no[450] more perfection, being for the prefent enforced to fende home titles rather then lawes, Propofitions rather then refolutions, Attemptes then Acchievements, hoping their courtefy will accepte our poore indevour, and their wifedome wilbe[451] ready to fupporte the weaknes of this little flocke.

Thirdly, the General Affembly doth humbly befeech[452] the faid Treafurer,[453] Counfell & Company, that albeit it belongeth to them onely to allowe or to abrogate any lawes w[ch] we fhall here make,[454] and that it is their right fo to doe,[455] yet that it would please them not to take it in ill parte if thefe lawes w[ch] we have nowe brought to light, do paffe currant[456] & be of force till fuche time as we[457] may knowe their farther pleafure out of Englande: for otherwife this people (who nowe at length have gotte[458] the raines[459] of former fervitude into their owne fwindge) would in fhorte time growe fo infolent, as they would fhake off all government, and there would be no living among them.

Their laft humble fuite is,[460] that the faid Counfell & Company would be pleafed, fo foon as they fhall finde[461] it convenient, to make

---

[442]regard to, McDonald; regard, Bancroft. [443]comanded, McDonald, Bancroft. [444]Trefurer, McDonald, Bancroft. [445]in, Bancroft. [446]therein, McDonald. [447]part, McDonald. [448]woulde eafily be found, McDonald; would eafily be founde, Bancroft. [449]fhort, McDonald. [450]no, omitted by McDonald. [451]will be, McDonald, Bancroft. [452]befeeche, McDonald. [453]Trefurer, McDonald. [454]inacte, McDonald, Bancroft. [455]righte foe to do, McDonald; right fo to doe, Bancroft. [456]current, Bancroft. [457]wee, McDonald, [458]gott, McDonald; got, Bancroft. [459]reines, McDonald; raines, Bancroft. [460]suit, McDonald. [461]find, McDonald.

good their promife fett downe[462] at the conclufion of their comiffion for eftablifhing the Counfel[463] of Eftate & the General[464] Affembly, namely, that they will give us power to allowe or difallowe of their orders of Courte, as his Ma^ty [465] hath given them power to allowe or to reject[466] our lawes.

In fume Sir George Yeardley, the Governo^r [467] prorogued the faid General[468] Affembly till the firfte of Marche, which is to fall out this prefent yeare of 1619, and in the mean feafon diffolved the fame.

FINIS.

I certify that the foregoing is a true and authentic copy taken from the volume above named.

JOHN McDONAGH,
Record Agent.
July 14th, 1871.

———

The McDonald copy has the following after Finis:

(in Dorfo.)

1619.
The proceedings of the firft Affembly of Virginia. July 1619.
True Copy,
AUGUSTUS AUSTEN BURT.

---

[462]down, McDonald.   [463]Counfell, McDonald, Bancroft.   [464]Generall, McDonald.   [465]Majefty, Mc-Donald; Ma^ty, Bancroft.   [466]rejecte, McDonald, Bancroft.   [467]Gover^nr, McDonald; Governour, Bancroft.   [468]Generall, McDonald.

LISTS

Livinge & the Dead in Virginia

February 16, 1623.

EDITORS' NOTE.

The paper from which this document is printed is to be found in the first volume of the McDonald papers. It is such a census of the inhabitants of the colony as the historical student would like to see made out at several other periods of our colonial history. We can find no legal enactment requiring such a census to be taken, and no order to that effect, save in the Instructions to Governor Wyatt, dated 24th July, 1621, where, among other things, he is directed "To make a catalogue of the people in every plantation, and their conditions; and of deaths, marriages and christenings."—Hening, Vol. I., p. 115.

The entries are as brief as possible, no middle names are given, and foreigners are entered according to nationality, or not more than one name allowed them. Not the least curious is the small number of negroes. Rolfe states, "About the last of August (1619) came in a Dutch man of warre that sold us twenty Negors" (Stith, p. 126), and nearly five years after, when this census was taken, there were but twenty-two in the Colony.

STATE PAPER OFFICE. ⎫
COLONIAL. ⎬
Volume 3, No. 2. ⎭

LISTS OF THE LIVINGE & DEAD IN VIRGINIA

Feb. 16th, 1623.

A LIST OF THE LIVINGE.

*At the Colledg Land.**

Thomas Marlett,	David Williams,
Chriftopher Branch,	William Walker,
Francis Boot,	Edward Hobfon,
William Browning,	Thomas Hobfon,
Walter Cooper,	John Day,
William Welder,	William Cookfey,
Leonard More,	Robert Farnell,
Daniell Shurley,	Nicholas Chapman,
Peeter Jorden,	Mathew Edlow,
Nicholas Perfe,	William Price,
William Dalbie,	Gabriell Holland,
Ifaias Rawton,	John Wattfon,
Theoder Moifes,	Ebedmeleck Gaftrell,
Robert Champer,	Thomas Ofborne.
Thomas Jones,	29

* *The Colledge Land.*—In "1619 Sir Edwin Sandys moved and obtained that ten thousand acres of land should be laid off for the University at Henrico, a place formerly resolved on for that purpose. This was intended as well for the colledge for the education of the Indians as also to lay the foundation of a seminary of learning for the English."—Stith, London ed., p. 163.

"On the northerly fide of James river, from the falls down to Henrico, containing ten miles in length, are the public lands referved and laid out, whereof ten thoufand are for the Univerfity lands, three thoufand are for the company's lands, with other lands belonging to the College."—MS. in the McDonald paper, entiled "Particulars of Land in Virginia," which was made out in 1625 or '6, the communication of the Governor in which he informs their lordships that he sends it, being dated May 17, 1626. McDonald papers, Vol. I., pp. 295–307.

At the first meeting of the Burgesses (1619) the College had no representative, but at the meeting held Oct. 16, 1629, the Burgesses "For the plantations at the Colledge were Leftn't Thomas Ofborne and Mathew Edlowe," whose names are in the text. See Hening, Vol. I., p. 138.

Att the Neak of Land.*

Luke Boys,
Mrs. Boys,
Robert Halam,
Jofeph Royall,
John Dods,
Mrs. Dods,
Elizabeth Perkinfon,
William Vincent,
Mrs. Vincent,
Allexander Bradwaye,
  his wife Bradwaye,
John Price,
  his wife Price,
Robert Turner,
Nathaniell Reeve,
Serjeant William Sharp,
Mrs. Sharp,
Richard Rawfe,
Thomas Sheppy,
William Clemens,
Ann Woodley,

Thomas Harris,
  his wife Harris,
Margaret Berman,
Thomas Farmer,
Hugh Hilton,
Richard Taylor,
  uxor Taylor,
Jofhua Chard,
Chriftopher Browne,
Thomas Oage,
  uxor Oage,
  infant Oage,
Henry Coltman,
Hugh Price,
  uxor Price,
  infant Price,
Mrs. Coltman,
Robert Greene,
  uxor Greene,
  infant Greene.

Att West & Sherlow Hundred.†

John Harris,
Dorothe Harris,
Infants { Harris,
        { Harris,

Thomas Floyd,
Ellias Longe,
William Nichollas,
Roger Ratcliffe,   78

---

* *Neak of Land.*—" There is another divifion of the country into necks of land, which are the bound-aries of the Efcheators, viz: the Northern Neck, between the Patowmeck and Rappahannock rivers.

"The neck between Rappahannock and York rivers, within which Pamunkey Neck is included.

"The neck between York and James rivers," &c., &c.—Beverly, Book IV., chap. ii.

This list being made up at James city this neck might be the one nearest to that place, and therefore the last one named by Beverly would be the one referred to; but inasmuch as in this ms. list it follows immediately after the College land, and in the list of Burgesses for 1629, occupies the same position, it is not improbable that it refers to the peninsula opposite Henrico, known on all the maps of the State as Farrar's island, and which has been made an island in reality by the completion of the canal begun by the United States army during the late civil war and afterwards finished by the engineer department of the same, under the direction of Col. W. P. Craighill. Hening reports Serit Sharpe a Burgess for this place in 1629, and Serjeant William Sharp is named in the text as living there in 1626.

† *West & Sherlow Hundred.*—Sir Thomas Dale annexed to New Bermuda "many miles of cham-pion and wood land ground in several hundreds, by the names of Nether Hundred, Shirley Hundred," &c.—Stith, p. 124–'5; Smith, General Hiftorie, 1627, p. 111. Hening names Burgesses (1629) from Shirley Hundred island and Shirley Hundred maine, and among the latter is the name of John Harris, which appears in the text.—Hening Vol. I., p. 138.

The name of Shirley appears on the Fry and Jefferson map only at the place where the same is now

Robert Milver,
Robert Parttin,
Margaret Parttin,
infantes { Parttin,
          { Parttin,
Henry Benfon,
Nicholas Blackman,
Nathanell Tattam,
Mathew Glofter,
Symon Surgis,
Nicholas Baley,
Ann Bayley,
Eliner Phillips,
Thomas Paulett,
Thomas Baugh,
Thomas Packer,
Jonas Bayley,
John Truffell,
Chriftopher Beane,

John Cartter,
Henry Bagwell,
Thomas Bagwell,
Edward Gardiner,
Richard Biggs,
Mrs. Biggs,
William Biggs, ⎱
Thomas Biggs, ⎬ Sons.
Richard Biggs, ⎰
William Afkew,
Henry Carman,
Andrew Dudley,
James Gay,
Anthony Burrows,
Rebecca Roffe,
sons { Roffe,
     { Roffe,
Petters, a maid.

*Att Jordan's Jorney.**

Sifelye Jordan,
Temperance Bayliffe,
Mary Jordan,
Margery Jordan,
William Farrar,
Thomas Williams,
Roger Prefton,
Thomas Brookes,
John Peede,
John Freme,
Richard Johnfon,
William Dawfon,
John Hely,
Robert Mannell,
Ann Linkon,
William Beffe,

Mrs. Beffe,
Chriftopher Saford,
uxor Saford,
John Caminge,
Thomas Palmer,
Mrs. Palmer,
fil Palmer,
Richard Englifh,
Nathaniel Caufey,
Mrs. Caufey,
Lawrence Evans,
Edward Clarke,
uxor Clarke,
infant Clarke,
John Gibbs,
John Davies,

147

---

located, opposite Bermuda Hundred, and well known as the residence of Hill Carter, Esq. A short distance below is an island not named on that map, but on modern maps as Eppes island, which we may presume was Shirley island. We do not find the name of West in the connection except in a paper entitled John Rolfe's relation to the State of Virginia, written in 1616, in which we learn that West and Shirley Hundred was about thirty-seven miles above James citie, which corresponds with the location above named. See Virginia Historical Register, Vol. I., p. 110.

* *Jordan's Jorney.*—Hening reports William Popkton as Burgess for this place. I do not find it on Fry and Jefferson's map, but Jordan's Point is there, and this is situated a short distance below City Point and is well known by the same name at the present time.

William Emerſon,
Henry Williams,
 uxor Williams,
Henry Fiſher,
 uxor Fiſher,

infant Fiſher,
Thomas Chapman
 uxor Chapman,
infant Chapman,
Edith Hollis,

Att Flourdieu Hundred.

Richard Gregory,
Edward Alborn,
Thomas Dellimager,
Thomas Hack,
Anthony Jones,
Robert Guy,
William Strachey,
John Browne,
Annis Boult,
William Baker,
Theoder Beriſton,
Walter Blake,
Thomas Watts,
Thomas Doughty,
George Deverell,
Richard Spurling,
John Woodſon,
William Straimge,
Thomas Dune,
John Landman,
Leonard Yeats,
George Levet,
Thomas Harvay,
Thomas Filenſt,
Robert Smith,
Thomas Garmder,
Thomas Gaſkon,
John Olives,
Chriſtopher Pugett,
Robert Peake,
Edward Tramorden,
Henry Linge,

Gibert Pepper,
Thomas Mimes,
John Linge,
John Gale,
Thomas Barnett,
Roger Thompſon,
Ann Thompſon,
Ann Doughty,
Sara Woodſon,
  Negors,
  Negors,
6 Negors,
  Negors,
  Negors,
  Negors,
Grivell, Pooley, Miniſter,
Samuel Sharp,
John Upton,
John Wilſon,
Henry Rowinge,
Nathaniell Thomas,
William Barrett,
Robert Okley,
Richard Bradſhaw,
Thomas Sawell,
John Bramford,
Anthony,⎫
William, ⎬ Negors men.
John,   ⎪
Anthony, ⎭
A Negors Woman.   224

*The rest at West and Sherlow Hundred Island.**

Capt Fackt Maddeſon,
Mary Maddeſon,

Thomas Wattſon,
James Wattſon,

<hr>

* *West and Sherlow Hundred Island.*—The distinction here made seems to confirm the suggestion contained in note to West and Sherlow Hundred,

Francis Weſt,
Roger Lewis,
Richard Domelow,
William Hatfeild,
Thomas Foſſett,
Ann Foſſett,
Jenkin Oſborne,
William Siſmore,
Martha Siſmore,
Stephen Braby,

Elizabeth Braby,
Edward Temple,
Daniel Vergo,
William Tathill, boy,
Thomas Haile, boy,
Richard Morewood,
Edward Sparſhott,
Barnard Jackſon,
William Brocke,
James Mayro.

At Chaplain's Choise.*

Iſacke Chaplaine,
Mrs. Chaplaine,
John Chaplaine,
Walter Prieſt,
William Weſton,
John Duffy,
Ann Michaell,
Thomas Phillipps,
Henry Thorne,
Robert Hudſon,
Iſacke Baugton,
Nicholas Sutton,

William Whitt,
Edward Butler,
Henry Turner,
Thomas Leg,
John Browne,
John Trachern,
Henry Willſon,
Thomas Baldwin,
Allexander Sanderſon,
David Ellis,
Sara More,
Ann, a maid.

Att James citie and within the Corporation thereof.†

Sir Francis Wyatt, Govr
Margarett, Lady Wyatt,
Hant Wyatt, miniſter,
Kathren Spencer,
Thomas Hooker,
John Gather,
John Matcheman,
Edward Cooke,

George Nelſon,
George Hall,
Lane Burtt,
Elizabeth Powell,
Mary Woodward,
Sir George Yeardley, knight,
Temperance Lady Yeardley,
Argall Yeardley,   284

---

* *Chaplain's Choise.*—This place and Jordan's Journey were represented in 1629, by Walter Price, according to Hening, and with only a fair allowance for the orthographical inaccuracies of the time and of different copyists, it is not impossible that the Walter Priest of the text is the same person. I can find no clue to its location, but it is reasonable to suppose it was near Jordan's Point.

† *James Citie.*—This birthplace of our State, eighty miles below Richmond, is now the property of a gentleman of New York city, who has the ground cultivated. During the war the soil was thrown up into fortifications, and pieces of armor, sword hilts, calthorps, gold, silver and copper coins were found. All that remains of the city is a portion of the brick tower which belonged to the church, and which attracts the attention of travellers on the river with an interest similar to that of Mount Vernon on the Potomac. Though visited by very few persons, yet the relic-hunters have removed all of the tombstones, and have attacked what remains of the church tower.

Frances Yeardley,
Elizabeth Yeardley,
Kilibett Hitchcocke,
Auften Combes,
John Fofter,
Richard Arrundell,
Sufan Hall,
Ann Grimes,
Elizabeth Lyon,
—— Younge,
negro ⎱ women,
negro ⎰
Alice Davifon, *vidua*,
Edward Sharples,
Jone Davies,   ·
George Sands, Treaf^r ,
Capt. William Perce,
Joan Perce,
Robert Hedges,
Hugh Win,
Thomas Moulfton,
Henry Farmer,
John Lightfoote,
Thomas Smith,
Roger Ruefe,
Allexander Gill,
John Cartwright,
Robert Auftine,
Edward Bricke,
William Ravenett,
Jocomb Andrews,
    uxor Andrews,
Richard Alder,
Efter Evere,
Angelo, a negar,
Doctor John Pott,
Elizabeth Pott,
Richard Townfend,
Thomas Leifter,
John Kullaway,
Randall Howlett,
Jane Dickinfon,
Fortune Taylor,
Capt. Roger Smith,
Mrs. Smith,
Elizabeth Salter,

Sara Macocke,
Elizabeth Rolfe,
Chriftopher Lawfon,
    uxor Em. Lawfon,
Francis Fouler,
Charles Waller,
Henry Booth,
Capt. Raph Hamor,
Mrs. Hamor,
Joreme Clement,
Elizabeth Clement,
Sara Langley,
Sifely Greene,
Ann Addams,
Elkinton Ratclife,
Francis Gibfon,
James Yemanfon,
John Pountes,
Chriftopher Beft,
Thomas Clarke,
Mr. Reignolds,
Mr. Hickmore,
    uxor Hickmore,
Sara Ruddell,
Edward Blaney,
Edward Hudfon,
    uxor Hudfon,
William Hartley,
John Shelley,
Robert Bew,
William Ward,
Thomas Mentis,
Robert Whitmore,
Robert Channtree,
Robert Sheppard,
William Sawyer,
Lanflott Danfport,
Mathew Loyd,
Thomas Ottway,
Thomas Crouth,
Elizabeth Starkey,
Elinor,
Mrs. Perry,
    infant Perry,
Frances Chapman,
George Graues,

uxor Graues,
Rebecca Snowe,
Sara Snowe,
John Ifgrane,
Mary Aftombe, *vidua*,
Benamy Bucke,
Gercyon Bucke,
Peleg Bucke,
Mara Bucke,
Abram Porter,
Brigett Clarke,
Abigall Afcombe,
John Jackfon,
 uxor Jackfon,
Ephraim Jackfon,
Mr. John Burrows,
Mrs. Burrows,
Anthony Burrows,
John Cooke,
Nicholas Gouldfmith,
Elias Gaile,
Andrew Howell,
Ann Afhley,
John Southern,
Thomas Pafmore,
Andrew Ralye,
Nathaniel Jefferys,
 uxor Jefferys,
Thomas Hebbs,
Clement Dilke,
Mrs. Dilke,
John Hinton,
Richard Stephens,
Waffell Rayner,
 uxor Rayner,
John Jackfon,
Edward Price,
Often Smith,

Thomas Spilman,
Bryan Cawt,
George Minify,
Moyes Ston,
Capt. Holmes,
Mr. Calcker,
Mrs. Calcker,
 infant Calcker,
Peceable Sherwood,
Anthony Weft,
Henry Barker,
Henry Scott,
Margery Dawfe,
Mr. Cann (or Cam),
Capt. Hartt,
Edward Spalding,
 uxor Spalding,
 puer Spalding,
 puella Spalding,
John Helin,
 uxor Helin,
 puer Helin,
 infant Helin,
Thomas Graye,
 uxor Graye,
Jone Graye,
William Graye,
Richard Younge,
 uxor Younge,
Jone Younge,
Rendall Smallwood,
John Greene,
William Mudge,
Mrs. Sothey,
Ann Sothey,
Elin Painter,
Goodman Webb.

In the Maine.

Richard Atkins,
 uxor Atkins,
William Baker,
Edward Oliver,
Samuell Morris,

Robert Davis,
Robert Lunthorne,
John Vernie,
Thomas Wood,
Thomas Rees,

Michael Batt,
  uxor Batt,
  vidua Tindall,
Mr. Stafferton,
  uxor Stafferton,
John Fiſher,
John Rose,
Thomas Thornegood,
John Badſton,
Suſan Blackwood,
Thomas Rinſton (or f),
Robert Scottiſmore,
Roger Kid,
Nicholas Bullington,
Nicholas Marttin,
John Carter,
Chriſtopher Hall,
David Ellis,
  uxor Ellis,
John Frogmorton,
Robert Marſhall,
Thomas Snow (orig. Swnow),
John Smith,
Lawrance Smalpage,
Thomas Croffe,
Thomas Prichard,
Richard Crouch,
Chriſtopher Redhead,
Henry Booth,
Richard Carven,
  uxor Carven,
John Howell,
William Burtt,
William Stocker,
Nicholas Roote,
Sara Kiddall,
  infants { .Kiddall,
           Kiddall,
Edward Fiſher,
Richard Smith,

John Wolrich,
Mrs. Wolrich,
Jonathin Giles,
Chriſtopher Ripen,
Thomas Banks,
Frances Butcher,
Henry Daivlen,
Arthur Chandler,
Richard Sanders,
Thomas Helcott,
Thomas Hichcocke,
Griffine Greene,
Thomas Oſbourn,
Richard Downes,
William Laurell,
Thomas Jordan,
Edward Buſbee,
Henry Turner,
Joſhua Crew,
Robert Hutchinſon,
Thomas Jones,
  uxor Jones,
Reignold Morecocke,
  uxor Morecocke,
Richard Bridgewatter,
  uxor Bridgewatter,
Mr. Thomas Bun,
Mrs. Bun,
Thomas Smith,
Elizabeth Hodges,
William Kemp,
  uxor Kemp,
Hugh Baldwine,
  uxor Baldwine,
John Wilmoſe,
Thomas Doe,
  uxor Doe,
George Fryer,
  uxor Fryer,
Stephen Webb.

In James Island.

John Oſbourn,
  uxor Oſbourn,
George Pope,

Robert Cunſtable,
William Jones,
  uxor Jones,

John Johnſon,
  uxor Johnſon,
  infants { Johnſon,
          { Johnſon,
John Hall,
  uxor Hall,
William Cookſey,
  uxor Cookſey,
  infant Cookſey,
Alice Kean,
Robert Fitts,
  uxor Fitts,
John Reddiſh,
John Grevett,
  uxor Grevett,
John Weſt,

Thomas Weſt,
Henry Glover,
Goodman Stocks,
  uxor Stocks,
  infant Stocks,
Mr. Adams,
Mr. Leet,
William Spence,
  uxor Spence,
  infant Spence,
James Tooke,
James Roberts,
Anthony Harlow,
Sara Spence,
George Shurke,
John Booth & Robt. Bennett.

The Neck of Land.

Mr. Kingſmeale,
  uxor Kingſmeale,
  infants { Kingſmeale,
          { Kingſmeale,
Raph Griphin,
Frances Compton,
John Smith,
John Filmer,
Edward, a negro,
Thomas Sulley,
  uxor Sulley,
Thomas Harwood,
George Fedam,

Peter Staber,
Thomas Popkin,
Thomas Sides,
Richard Perſe,
  uxor Perſe,
Allen, his man,
Iſabell Pratt,
Thomas Allnutt,
  uxor Allnutt,
John Paine,
Roger Redes,
Elinor Sprad.

Over the River.

John Smith,
  uxor Smith,
  infant Smith,
John Pergo,
Richard Fenn,
William Richardſon,
Robert Lindſey,
Richard Dolfemb,
John Bottam,
John Elliott,
Suſan Barber,

Thomas Gates,
  uxor Gates,
Percevall Wood,
Anthony Burrin,
William Bedford,
William Sands,
John Proctor,
Mrs. Proctor,
Phettiplace Cloſe,
Henry Home,
Richard Home,

7

Thomas Flower,
William Bullocke,
Ellias Hinton,
John Foxen,
Edward Smith,
John Skimer,

Martine De Moone,
William Naile,
Thomas Fitts,
Elizabeth Abbitt,
Alice Fitts,

At the Plantation over against James Cittie.*

Capt. Samuel Mathews,
Benjamin Owin,
Rice Axʳ Williams,
John, a negro,
Walter Parnell,
William Parnell,
Margaret Roades,
John Weſt,
Francis Weſt, *vidua*,
Thomas Dayhurſt,
Robert Mathews,
Arthur Gouldſmith,
Robert Williams,
Morice Loyd,
Aron Conway,
William Sutton,
Richard Greene,
Mathew Haman,
Samuell Davies,
John Thomas,
John Docker,
Abram Wood,
Michaell Lupworth,
John Davies,
Lewis Baly,
James Daries,
Alice Holmes,
Henry Barlow,
Thomas Button,
Edmond Whitt,
Zacharia Criſpe,
John Burland,
Thomas Hawkins,

Thomas Phillips,
Paul Reinolds,
Nicholas Smith,
Elizabeth Williams,
Hugh Cruder,
Edward Hudſon,
Robert Sheppard,
Thomas Ottawell,
Thomas Crouth,
Robert Bew,
John Ruſſell,
Robert Chantry,
George Rodgers,
Lanſlott Damport,
John Shule,
Nathaniell Loyd,
William Sawyer,
William Ward,
William Hartley,
Jereme Whitt,
Livetenant Purfrey,
Edward Grindall,
Mr. Swift,
William Hames,
George Gurr,
Henry Wood,
John Baldwine,
John Needome,
William Bricks,
Nicholas Thompſon,
John Dency,
Eraſmus Cartter,
John Edwards,

704

---

* *At the Plantation over against James Citie.*—Hening reports as Burgesses (after James City) for the other side of the water, Capt. John West, Capt ffelgate; as John West's name appears in the text under this head, we presume the places are identical and refer to probably some place on the opposite side of the James river not more definitely designated.

George Bayley,
George Sparke,
Nicholas Comin,
Nicholas Arras,
Marttin Turner,
John Stone, infant,

Davy Mansfield,
John Denmarke,
Elizabeth Rutten,
Goodwife Bincks,
A fervant of Mr. Moorewood's.

The Glase Howse.*

Vincentio,
Bernardo,
Ould Sheppard, his fonn,

Richard Tarborer.
Mrs. Bernardo.

At Archur's Hoop.†

Lieutenant Harris,
Rowland Lottis,
  uxor Lottis,
John Elifon,
  uxor Elifon,
George Sanders,
Thomas Corder,

Jofeph Johnfon,
George Pran,
John Bottom,
Thomas Farley,
  uxor Farley,
  a child,
Nicholas Shotton.

At Hogg Island.‡

David Sanders, minifter,
John Utie,

Mrs. Utie,
John Utie, infant,   738

---

* *The Glass House.*—We find frequent references to but no notice of the erection of this building. Smith, in his account of the attempt to murder him by the Dutchmen in 1608, says, "They sent Francis, their companion, difguifed like a Salvage, to the Glaffe-houfe, a place in the woods neare a myle from Iames Toune," &c., Smith attempted to apprehend him, but he escaped, and after he had sent "20 fhot after him; himfelf returning from the Glaffe Houfe alone," when he encountered the king of the Paspa heigh whom he defeated and "led him prifoner to Iames Toune and put him in chaynes." Smith (1627) pp. 83, 84.

Stith says after the return of Newport from his expedition of discovery up James river "No sooner were they landed but the Prefident (Smith) difperfed as many as were able, fome to make Glafs and others for Pitch," &c.; and in 1609, "And now the Colony pursued their bufinefs with alacrity and fuccefs. They made three or four lafts of Tar, Pitch, and Soap ashes and produced a trial of glafs," &c., &c. And in 1621, speaking of the subscriptions opened in England, he says, "The third roll was for a glafs furnace to make beads, which was the current coin in the Indian trade; and one Captaine Norton, with fome Italian workmen, was fent over for that purpofe." See also Stith, pp. 95, 97, 197, 198. As the names of Vincentio and Benardo appear in the text, we may infer that some of the Italian workmen survived the massacre of 1622.

† *Archur's Hoop.*—Archer's Hope creek on Fry and Jefferson's map empties into James river but a short distance below Jamestown, and in the Particulars of Land in Virginia, referred to in note on page 37, Archer's Hope is named.

‡ *Hogg Island.*—This is set down on Smith's and all succeeding maps. It is six or eight miles below Jamestown island, and its name being unchanged, is very well known at the present time. In the text John Utie is named as one of the inhabitants, and his name appears in Hening as one of the Burgesses in 1629 from "the plantations between Archer's Hope and Martins Hundred," which corresponds with its location.

William Tyler,
Elizabeth Tyler,
Richard Whitby,
William Ramſhaw,
Rice Watkins,
Thomas Foſkew, loft,
Hener Elſword,
Thomas Cauſey,
George Union,
Henry Woodward,
Roger Webſter,
John Donſton,
Joſeph Johnſon,
Richard Crocker, child,

William Hitchcocke, loft,
George Prowſe,
Robert Parramore,
John Jarvice, als. Glover,
John Browne,
William Burcher,
John Burcher,
John Fulwood,
Thomas Branſby,
Thomas Colly,
Thomas Simpſon,
Thomas Powell,
Nicholas Longe,

At Martin's Hundred.*

William Harwood,
Samuell March,
Hugh Hues,
John Jackſon,
Thomas Ward,
John Stevans,
Humphrey Walden,
Thomas Doughtie,
John Haſley,
Samwell Weaver,
vidua Jackſon,
filia Jackſon,

Mrs. Taylor,
Ann Windor,
Elizabeth Bygrane,
Mr. Lake,
Mr. Burren,
John Stone,
Samwell Cultey,
John Helline,
   uxor Helline,
A Frenchman *et uxor*,
Thomas Siberg.

At Warwick Squrake.†

John Batt,
Henry Prinffe,
Waſſell Weblin,

Anthony Read,
Frances Woodſon,
Henry Phillips,   794

---

* *Martin's Hundred.*—Martin's Hundred is located on Fry and Jefferson's map between Hog island and Mulberry island, and on a small stream called Skies creek, on the north side of James river. In the proceedings of the Assembly in 1619 it is referred to as Paspaheigh's, alias Martin's Hundred, see ante p. 30 In the "Particulars of Land in Virginia," before mentioned, we read, "Martin's Hundred, containing 80,000 acres, part planted." Captaine Martin was made president by Capt. John Smith in 1609, but he did not desire the position and resigned. At the Assembly in 1619, he and the privileges named in his patent, and certain charges against him of unfair dealing with the Indians occupied no little attention.— See ante, pp. 12 and 13. For further particulars in regard to his attempts at imposition on the Company and like charges, the reader is referred to Stith, pp. 219, 220, 221.

† *Warwick Squrake.*—It is difficult to decide upon either the spelling or the pronunciation of this word. On Smith's map it is located on the south side of James river, and about fifteen or twenty miles below Jamestown, and is spelt Waraskorack, and on page 59 he spells it Waraskoyack; Fry and Jefferson locate

Petter Collins,
Chriftopher Reinolds,
Edward Mabin,
John Maldman,
Thomas Collins,
George Rufhmore,
Thomas Spencer,
George Clarke,
Richard Bartlett,
Francis Banks,
John Jenkins,
Thomas Jones,
William Denham,

Peter,
Anthony,
Frances,
Margrett, } negroes,
John Bennett,
Nicholas Skinner,
John Atkins,
John Pollentin,
Rachell Pollentin,
Margrett Pollentin,
Mary, a maid,
Henry Woodward,
Thomas Sawyer,
Thomas, a Boye.

At the Indian Thickett.

Henry Woodall,
Gregory Dory,
John Fofter,
John Greene,
John Ward,
Chriftopher Wendmile,

Richard Rapier,
Cutbert Pierfon,
Adam Rumell,
Richard Robinfon,
James, a French man.

At Elizabeth Cittye.*

Capt. Ifacke Whittakers,
Mary Whittakers,
Charles Atkinfon,
Charles Calthrop,
John Lankfeild,
Bridges Freeman,
Nicholas Wefell,
Edward Loyd,
Thomas North,
Anthony Middleton,

Richard Popely,
Thomas Harding,
William Joye,
Raph Ofborne,
Edward Barnes,
Thomas Thorugood,
Ann Atkinfon,
—— Lankfeild,
—— Medclalfe,
George Nuce,   852

it on Burwell's bay, and call it Warnicqueack. Stith calls it Warrasqueake, and gives an interesting account of "the King of that town," and his hospitable treatment of Capt. Smith on the night of the 29th of December, 1608: p. 85. In the "Particulars of Land," McDonald MS. above referred to, it is spelt as shown in the following extract: " Warofquoiacke Plantation conteyning downewardes from Hogg ifland, 14 miles by the ryver side," &c., &c., p. 313.

Hening has it Warrosquoiack, Vol. I., p. 149. In 1634 "the country divided into eight fhires," and this being one of them. Hening there spells it Warrosquyoake. Vol. I., p. 224.

* *Elizabeth Citty.*—The settlement which was the foundation of the county still known by the same name. It includes the peninsula formed by the Chesapeake bay and James river. At the meeting of the Burgesses in 1629 it was represented as two districts or burroughs, viz: the upper parte and the lower parte, each having three delegates, and the text shows that of these Thomas Willobouy of the upper and Adam Thoroughgood of the lower part were living there in 1626.

Elizabeth Whittakers,
George Roads,
Edward Joʃnfon (ʃic.),
  (qy. Johnʃon,)
William Fouller,
Reinold Goodwyn,
James Larmount,
John Jackʃon,
  vidua Johnʃon,
  vidua Fowler,
Two Frenchmen,
George Medcalfe,
Walter Ely,
Thomas Lane,
Barthelmew Hopkins,
John Jefferʃon,
Robert Threʃher,
John Rowes,
Mr. Yates,
Robert Goodman,
  uxor Ely,
  infant Ely,
Capt. Rawleigh Craʃhaw,

Robert Wright,
James Sleight,
John Welchman,
John More,
Henry Potter,
Mr. Rofwell,
William Gawntlett,
Oʃborne Smith,
  uxor More,
  uxor Wright,
  uxor Wright,
  filia Wright,
Thomas Dowʃe,
Samwell Bennett,
William Browne,
William Allen,
Lewis Welchman,
Robert More,
Mrs. Dowʃe,
  uxor Bennett,
  pueri { Bennett,
         { Bennett,

*At Bricke Row.**

Thomas Flint,
John Hampton,
Richard Peirʃby,
William Rookins,
Rowland Williams,
Steven Dixon,
Thomas Riʃby,
Henry Wheeler,
James Brooks,
Samuel Bennett,
John Carning,
Thomas Neares,
Robert Salvadge,
William Barry,
Joʃeph Hatfield,

Edward Marʃhall,
Ambroʃe Griffith,
Petter Arrundell,
Anthony Bonall, } Frenchmen,
—— La Geurd, }
James Bonall, a Frenchm.,
John Arrundell,
John Haine,
Nicholas Row,
Richard Althrop,
John Loyd,
  uxor Haine (or Hame),
  uxor Hampton,
Elizabeth Arrundell,
Margret Arrundell,   927

† *Bricke Row.*—I can find no reference to this place unless "The Row" on the north side of the James a short distance above the mouth of the Chichahominy, on Fry and Jefferson's map is the place.

At Bass's Choice.

Capt. Nathaniel Baffe,
Samwell Baffe,
Benjamin Simmes,
Thomas Sheward,
Benjamin Handcleare,
William Barnard,
John Shelley,
Nathaniell Moper,
Nath. Gammon,
Margrett Giles,

Richard Longe,
uxor Longe,
infant Longe,
Richard Evans,
William Newman,
John Army,
Peter Langden,
Henry,
Andrew Rawley,
Peter,

More at Elizabeth Cittie.

Lieutenant Sheppard,
John Powell,
John Wooley,
Cathren Powell,
John Bradfton,
Francis Pitts,
Gilbert Whitfield,
Peter Hereford,
Thomas Faulkner,
Efaw de la Ware,
William Cornie,
Thomas Curtife,
Robert Brittaine,
Roger Walker,
Henry Kerfly,
Edward Morgaine,
Anthony Ebfworth,
Agnes Ebfworth,
Elinor Harris,
Thomas Addifon,
William Longe,
William Smith,
William Pinfen,
Capt. William Tucker,
Capt. Nick Martean,
Leftenant Ed. Barkly,
Daniell Tanner,
John Morris,
George Thomfon,
Paule Thomfon,
William Thomfon,

Pafta Champin,
Stephen Shere,
Jeffery Hall,
Rich. Jones,
William Hutchinfon,
Richard Apleton,
Thomas Evans,
Wefton Browne,
Robert Mounday,
Steven Colloe,
Raph Adams,
Thomas Phillips,
Francis Barrett,
Mary Tucker,
Jane Brackley,
Elizabeth Higgins,
Mary Mounday,
Chouponke, an Indian,
Anthony, } negroes.
Ifabella, }
Lieut. Lupo,
Phillip Lupo,
Bartholmew Wetherfby,
Henry Draper,
Jofeph Haman,
Elizabeth Lupo,
Albiano Wetherfby,
John Laydon,
Ann Laydon,
Virginia Laydon,
Alice Laydon,

1009

Katherine Laydon,
William Evans,
William Julian,
William Kemp,
Richard Wither,
John Jornall,
Walter Mafon,
Sara Julian,
Sara Gouldocke,
John Salter,
William Soale,
Jeremy Dickenfon,
Lawrance Peele,
John Evans,
Marke Evans,
George Evans,
John Downeman,
Elizabeth Downeman,
William Baldwin,
John Sibley,
William Clarke,
Rice Griffine,
Jofeph Mofley,
Robert Smith,
John Cheefman,
Thomas Cheefman,
Edward Cheefman,
Peter Dickfon,
John Baynam,
Robert Sweet,
John Parrett,
William Fouks,
John Clackfon,
John Hill,
William Morten,
William Clarke,
Edward Stockdell,
Elizabeth Baynam,
George Davies,
Elizabeth Davies,
Ann Harrifon,
John Curtise,
John Walton,
Edward Ofton,
Toby Hurt,
Cornelius May,

Elizabeth May,
Henry May, child,
Thomas Willowbey,
Oliver Jenkinfon,
John Chandeler,
Nicholas Davies,
Jone Jenkins,
Mary Jenkins,
Henry Gouldwell,
Henry Prichard,
Henry Barber,
Ann Barber,
John Hutton,
Elizabeth Hutton,
Thomas Baldwin,
John Billiard,
Reynold Booth,
Mary,
Elizabeth Booth, child,
Capt. Thomas Davies,
John Davies,
Thomas Huges,
William Kildrige,
Alex^r Mountney,
Edward Bryan,
Percivall Ibotfon,
John Penrice,
Robert Locke,
Elizabeth & Ann Ibotfon,
Edward Hill,
Thomas Beft,
Hanna Hill,
Elizabeth Hill,
Robert Salford,
John Salford,
Phillip Chapman,
Thomas Parter,
Mary Salford,
Francis Chamberlin,
William Hill,
William Harris,
William Worldige,
John Forth,
Thomas Spilman,
Rebecca Chamberlin,
Alice Harris,   1102

Pharow Phlinton,
Arthur Smith,
Hugh Hall,
Robert Sabin,
John Cooker,
Hugh Dicken,
William Gayne,
Richard Mintren, Junr ,
Joane Hinton,
Elizabeth Hinton,
Rebecca Coubber,
Richard Mintren, Senr ,
John Frye,
William Brooks,
Sibile and William Brooks,
Thomas Crifpe,
Richard Packe,
Miles Prichett,
Thomas Godby,
Margery Prichett,
Jone Goodby,
Jone Grindry,
John Iniman,
Mary Grindry,
John Grindry, child,
John Waine,
Ann Waine,
Mary Ackland,
George Ackland,
John Harlow,
William Cappe,
Edward Watters,
Paule Harwood,
Nick. Browne,
Adam Througood,
Richard Eaft,
Stephen Read,
Grace Watters,
Willm Watters.
Willm Ganey,
Henry Ganey,
John Robinfon,
Robert Browne,
Thomas Parrifh,
Edmund Spalden,
Roger Farbracke,
8

Theodor Jones,
William Baldwin,
Luke Aden,
Anna Ganey,
Anna Ganey, *filia*,
Elizabeth Pope,
Rebecca Hatch,
Thomafin Loxmore,
Thomas Garnett,
Elizabeth Garnett,
Sufan Garnett,
Frances Michell,
Jonas Stockton,
Timothee Stockton,
William Cooke,
Richard Boulten,
Frances Hill,
John Jackfon,
Richard Davies,
Ann Cooke,
Dictras Chrifmus,
Thomas Hill,
Arthur Davies,
William Newcome,
Elizabeth Chrifmus,
Joan Davies,
Thomas Hetherfall,
William Douglas,
Thomas Douthorn,
Elizabeth Douthorn,
Samuel Douthorn, a boy,
Thomas, an Indian,
John Hazard,
Jone Hazard,
Henry,
Frances Mafon,
Michaell Wilcocks,
William Querke,
Mary Mafon,
Mandlin Wilcocks,
Mr. Keth, minifter,
John Bufh,
John Cooper,
Jonadab Illett,
John Barnaby,
John Seaward,

Robest Newman,
William Parker,
Thomas Snapp,

Clement Evans,
Thomas Spilman,
Thomas Parrifh.

At the Eastern Shore.

Capt. William Epps,
Mrs. Epps,
Peter Epps,
William,
Edmond Cloake,
William Bribby,
Thomas Cornifh,
John Fifher,
William Dry,
Henry Wilfon,
Peter Porter,
Chriftopher Cartter,
John Sunnfill (or Sumfill),
Nicholal Graunger,
James Vocat Piper,
Edward,
John,
Thomas,
George,
Charles Farmer,
James Knott,
John Afcomb,
Robert Fennell,
Phillip,
Daniell Cogley,
William Andrews,
Thomas Granes,
John Wilcocks,
Thomas Crampe,
William Coomes,
John Parfons,
John Coomes,
James Chambers,
Robert Ball,
Goodwife Ball,
Thomas Hall,
Ifmale Hills,
John Tyers,

Walter Scott,
Goodwife Scott,
Robert Edmonds,
Thomas Hichcocke,
John Evans,
Henry Wattkins,
Peregree Wattkins,
Daniell Watkins,
John Blower,
Gody Blower,
John,
A boy of Mr. Cans,
John How,
John Butterfeild,
William Davies,
Peter Longman,
John Wilkins,
Goodwife Wilkins,
Thomas Powell,
Gody Powell,
Thomas Parke,
William Smith,
Edward Drew,
Nicholas Hofkins,
  and his child,
William Williams,
Mrs. Williams,
John Throgmorton,
Bennanine Knight,
Chad Gunfton,
Abram Analin,
Thomas Blacklocke,
John Barnett,
Thomas Savadge,
William Beane,
Salamon Greene,
John Wafborne,
William Quills.

1277

The End of the List of the Living.

A LIST OF THE NAMES OF THE DEAD IN VIRGINIA

SINCE APRIL LAST.

FEBʸ 16ᵗʰ, 1623.

Colledge.

William Lambert,

John Wood,
William More, } killed,

Thomas Naylor,
James Howell. } killed,

At the Neck of Land.

Moſes Conyers,
George Grimes,
William Clements,

Thomas Fernley, killed,
Edward.

At Jordain's Jorney.

Roger Much,
Mary Reefe,
Robert Winter,
Robert Woods,

Richard Shriefe,
Thomas Bull,
John Kinton,
Daniell,

At West & Sherlow Hundred.

Samwell Foreman,
Zorobabell,
2 Indians,
One negar,
Thomas Roberts,

John Edmonds,
John Laſey,
Daniell Francke,
Capt. Nath. Weſt,
Chriſtopher Harding, killed.

At Flower de Hundred.

John Mayor,
William Waycome,
Thomas Priſe,
Robert Walkin,
John Fetherſton,

John Ax. Roberts,
Richard Jones,
Richard Griffin,
Richard Ranke,
William Edger,

39

John Fry,
Dixi Carpenter,
William Smith,
James Cindnare,

Edward Temple,
Sara Salford,
John Stanton,
Chrifto. Evans.

At James Cittie.

Mr. Sothey,
John Dumpont,
Thomas Browne,
Henry Sothey,
Thomas Sothey,
Mary Sothey,
Elizabeth Sothey,
Thomas Clarke,
Margarett Shrawley,
Richard Walker,
Vallentyne Gentler,
Peter Brifhitt,
Humphrey Boyfe,
John Watton,
Arthur Edwards,
Thomas Fifher,
William Spence, ⎫ loft,
Mrs. Spence, ⎭
George Sharks,
John Bufh,
Mr. Collins,
  uxor Collins,
Mr. Peyden,
Peter De Maine,
Goodman Afcomb,
Goodman Witts,
William Kerton,
Mr. Atkins,
Thomas Hakes,
Peter Gould,
Robert Ruffe,
Ambrofe Frefey,
Henry Fry,
John Dinfe,
Thomas Trundall,
Richard Knight,
John Jefferys,
John Hamun,
John Meridien,

John Countivane,
Thomas Guine,
Thomas Somerfall,
William Rowfley,
Elizabeth Rowfley,
  a maid of theirs,
Robert Bennett,
Thomas Roper,
Mr. Fitziefferys,
Mrs. Smith,
Peter Martin,
James Jakins,
Mr. Crapplace,
John Lullett,
Ann Dixon,
William Howlett,
Mr. Furlow's child,
Jacob Prophett,
John Reding (or Reeing)
Ritchard Atkins,
  his child,
John Bayly,
William Jones, his fon and,
John, Mr. Pearis' fervant,
Jofias Hartt,
Judith Sharp,
Ann Quarle,
—— Reignolds,
William Dier,
Mary Dier,
Thomas Sexton,
Mary Brawdrye,
Edward Normanfell,
Henry Fell,
—— Enims,
Roger Turnor,
Thomas Guine,
John Countway,
John Meriday,   125

Benjamine Uſher,
John Haman,
John Jefferyes,
Richard Knight,
John Walker,
Hoſier,

William Jackſon,
William Apleby,
John Manby,
Arthur Cooke,
Stephen.

At the Plantation over ag^t James Cittie.

Humphrey Clough,
Morris Chaloner,
Samuell Betton,
John Gruffin,
William Edwards,
Wiliam Saliſbury,
Mathew Griffine,
Robert Adwards,
John Jones,
Thomas Prichard,
Thomas Morgaine,
Thomas Biggs,
Nicholas Buſhell,
Robert Williams,
Robert Reynolds,
Edward Huies,
Thomas Foulke,
Mathew Jenings,
Richard Morris,
Frances Barke,
John Ewins,
Samwell Fiſher,
John Ewins,
James Cartter,
Edward Fletcher,
Aderton Greene,
Morice Baker,
Robert, Mr. Ewins' man,
Robert Pidgion,
Thomas Triggs,
James Thurſby,
Nicholas Thimbleby,
Frances Millett,

John Hooks,
Thomas Lawſon,
William Miller,
Nicholas Fatrice,
John Champ,
John Maning,
Richard Edmonds,
David Collins,
Thomas Guine,
John Vicars,
John Meredie,
Beng. Uſher,
John Cantwell,
Richard Knight,
Robert Hellue,
Thomas Barrow,
John Enines,
Edward Price,
Robert Taylor,
Richard Butterey,
Mary Lacon,
Robert Baines,
Joſeph Arther,
Thomas Maſon,
John Beman,
Chriſto. Pittman,
Thomas Willer,
Samwell Fulſhaw,
John Walmſley,
Abram Colman,
John Hodges,
Naamy Boyle,

At Hogg Island.

William Brakley,
Peter Dun,

John Long.

At Martin's Hundred.

Henry Bagford,
Nicholas Gleadſton,
Nicholas Dornigton,
Raph Rogers,
Richard Frethram,
John Brogden,
John Beanam,
Francis Atkinſon,
Robert Atkinſon,
John Kerill,
Edward Davies,
Percivall Mann,
Mathew Staneling,
Thomas Nicholls,

2 children of the Frenchmen,
John Pattiſon, ⎱ killed,
   uxor Pattiſon, ⎰
Edward Windor,
Thomas Horner,
John Walker,
Thomas Pope,
Richard Ston,
John Cateſby,
Richard Stephens,
William Harris,
Chriſto. Woodward,
Joſeph Turner.

At Warwick Squrake.

Joſias Collins,
Clement Wilſon,
William Robinſon,
Chriſto. Rawſon,
Thomas Winſlow,
   uxor Winſlow,
   infant Winſlow,
Alexʳ Suffames,
Thomas Prickett,
Thomas Maddox,
John Greene,
Nathaniel Stanbridg,
John Litton,

Chriſto. Aſh,
   uxor Aſh,
   infant Aſh,
Nethaniel Lawe, ⎱ killed,
Jane Fiſher, ⎰
Phillip Jones,
Edward Banks,
John Symons,
Thomas Smith,
Thomas Griffin,
George Cane,
Robert Whitt,
Symon, an Italien.

At Elizabeth Cittíe.

Charle Marſhall,
William Hopkicke,
Dorothie Parkinſon,
William Robertts,
John Farrar,
Martin Cuffe,
Thomas Hall,
Thomas Smith,
Chriſto. Robertts,
Thomas Browne,
Henry Fearne,

Thomas Parkins,
Mr. Huffy,
James Collis,
Raph Rockley,
William Geales,
George Jones,
Andrew Allinſon,
William Downes,
Richard Gillett,
Goodwife Nonn,
Hugo Smale,

Thomas Winterfall,
John Wright,
James Fenton,
Cifely, a maid,
John Gavett,
James, } Irifhmen,
John, }
Jocky Armeftronge,
Wolfton Pelfant,
Sampfon Pelfant,
Cathrin Capps,
William Elbridg,
John Sanderfon,
John Bewbricke,
John Baker, killed,
William Lupo,
Timothy Burley,
Margery Frifle,
Henry Weft,
Jafper Taylor,
Brigett Searle,
Anthony Andrew,
Edmond Cartter,
Thomas ——,
William Gauntlett,
Gilbert ——, killed,
Chriftopher Welchman,
John Hilliard,
Gregory Hilliard,
John Hilliard,
William Richards,
Elizabeth, a maid,
Capt. Hickcocke,
Thomas Keinnfton,
Capt. Lincolne,
Chad. Gulftons,
   uxor Gulftons,
   infant Gulftons,
George Cooke,
Richard Goodchild,

Chrifenus, his child,
Elizabeth Mafon,
Symon Wither,
Whitney Guy,
Thomas Brodbanke,
William Burnhoufe,
John Sparkes,
Robert Morgaine,
John Locke,
William Thompfon,
Thomas Fulham,
Cutberd Brooks,
Innocent Poore,
Edward Dupper,
Elizabeth Davies,
Thomas Buwen,
Ann Barber,
William Lucott,
Nicholas ——, killed,
Henry Bridges,
Henry Payton,
Richard Griffin,
Raph Harrifon,
Samwell Harvie,
John Boxer,
Benjaimine Boxer,
Thomas Servant,
Frances Chamberline,
Bridgett Dameron,
Ifarell Knowles,
Edward Bendige,
William Davies,
John Phillips,
Daniell Sandwell,
William Jones,
Robert Ball's wife,
Robert Leaner,
Hugh Nickcott,
John Knight.

Out of the Ship called The Furtherance.

John Walker,
—— Hofier,
William Jackfon,

William Apleby,
John Manby,
Arthur Cooke.
Steven,

366

Out of the God's Gift.

Mr. Clare, mafter,   Wllliam Bennett.

Out of the Margrett & John.

Mr. Langley,   Mr. Wright.

The Guner of the *William & John.*   371

FINIS.

EDITOR'S NOTE.

The reader will perceive that the foregoing list of the dead reports only those who had died " since April last" (1622), consequently does not include the victims of the Indian massacre, which occurred on the 22d of March of that year. The number which fell by that diabolical conspiracy, as reported by Smith, amounted to 347, and in his Generall Historie, at page 149, he has a list of the numbers murdered at different places. Neil copies from the Records of the Virginia Company (now in the Congressional Library at Washington) a list of their names—see his "History of the Virginia Company," pp. 339–346—and considering that it is proper to annex this to the list preceding we herewith give it. The total corresponds with the statement in Smith's Historie.

The number of deaths in the census list shows a mortality amounting in one year to upwards of twenty per cent. of the whole population, exceeding the number which fell in the massacre by twenty-four. The fullest details of this and many other matters relating to the Colony while under the Virginia Company, can be found more fully shown in Neil's History of the Virginia Company than in any other work we have seen.

"Here following is fet downe a true lift of the names of all thofe that were maffacred by the treachery of the Sauages in Virginia, the 22ⁿᵈ March laft.

"To the end that their lawfull heyres may take fpeedy order for the inheritinge of their lands and eftates there. For which the honourable Company of Virginia are ready to do them all right and fauour:"

At Captaine Berckley's Plantation, seated at Falling Creeke, some 66 miles from James Citie, in Virginia.

John Berkley, Efquire,
Thomas Brafington,
John Sawyer,
Roger Dauid,
Francis Gowfh,
Bartholmew Peram,
Giles Peram,
John Dowler,
Laurence Dowler,
Lewis Williams,
Richard Bafcough,
Thomas Holland,

John Hunt,
Robert Horner Mafon,
Phillip Barnes,
William Swandal,
Robert Williams, his Wife and Childe,
Giles Bradfhawe, his Wife and Childe,
John Howlet and his fonne,
Thomas Wood and Collins his man,
Jofeph Fitch, apothecary to Doctor Pots.

9

At Master Thomas Sheffield Plantation, some three miles from the Falling Creeke.

Mafter Th: Sheffield[1] and Rachel his wife,
John Reeue,
William Tyler, a boy,
Samuel Reeue,
John Ellen,
Robert Tyler, a boy,

Mathew ———,
Judeth Howard,
Thomas Poole,
Methufalem ———,
Thomas Taylor,
William Tyler.

At Henrico Iland, about two miles from Sheffield's Plantation.

——— Atkins,
——— Wefton,
Philip Shatford,

William Perigo,
Owen Jones, one of Capt. Berk-ley's people.

Slaine of the Colledge People, about two miles from Henrico-Citie.

Samuel Stringer,
George Soldan,
William Baffet,
John Perry,
Edward Ember,
Jarrat Moore,

Thomas Xerles,
Thomas Freeman,
John Allen,
Thomas Cooke,
John Clements,
James Faulkoner,

Chriftopher Henley,
William Jordan,
Robert Dauis,
Thomas Hobfon,
William Bailey.

At Apo-mattucke River, at Mafter Abraham Pierce his Plantation, some five miles off the Colledge People.

William Charte,
Jo: Waterhowfe,

John Barker, a boy,
Robert Yeoman.

At Charles-Citie and about the precincts of Capt. Smith's Company.

Roger Royal,
Thomas Jones,

Robert Maruel,
Edward Heydon,

Henry Bufhel.

At other Plantations next adioyning.

Richard Plat and his Brother,
Henry Milward, his wife, his Childe and his Sifter,

Richard, a boy,
Goodwife Redhead.

At Mr. William Farrar's House.

Mafter John England and his man,
John Bel,
Henricke Peterfon and Alice, his Wife, and William, her fonne,

Thomas, his man,
James Woodfhaw,
Mary and ⎫
Elizabeth, ⎭ Maid fervants.

———
[1] The son of William Sheffield.

At Berkley-Hundred, some five miles from Charles-Citie.

Capt. George Sharpe, Efq., one of his Maiefties Pentioners.
John Rowles,
Richard Rowles, his Wife and Childe,
Giles Wilkins,
Giles Bradway,
Richard Fereby,
Thomas Sharpe,
Robert Jordan,
Edward Painter,

At Westouer, about a mile from Berkley-Hundred.

And Firft at Cap. Fr. Weft's Plantation:
James Englifh,   Richard Dafh.

At Mafter John Weft's Plantation:
Chriftopher Turner,   Dauid Owen.

At Capt. Nathanael Wefts:
Michael Aleworth,   John Wright.

At Lieutenant Gibs his Dividend:
John Paly,
Thomas Ratcliffe,
Michael Booker,
John Higglet,
Nathanael Earle,
John Gibbes,
William Parker,
Richard Wainham,
Benomy Keyman,
Thomas Gay,
James Vpfall,
Daniel, Mr Dombelowes man.

At Mr. Richard Owen's Houfe:
Richard Owen,
Stephen Dubo,
Francis, an Irifhman,
Thomas Paine,
One old Maid called blinde Margaret,
William Reeue,

At Mafter Owen Macar's Houfe:
Owen Macar,
Garret Farrel,
Richard Yeaw,
One Boy.

At Mafter Macock's Dividen:
Capt. Samuel Macock, Efquire,
Edward Lifter,
Thomas Browne,
John Downes.

At Flowerdieu-Hundred, Sir George Yeardley's Plantation.

John Philips,
Thomas Nufon,
John Braford,
Robert Taylor,
Samuel Jarret,
Elizabeth Bennet.

At the other side of the River, opposite to Flowerdieu-Hundred.

Mafter Hobfon and his wife,
Richard Storks,
John Slaughter,

Thomas Philips,
Richard Campion,
Anne Greene.

At Mr. Swinhowe his House.

Miftris Swinhow and Thomas and
    George Swinhow, her fonnes,
Richard Moffe,

John Larkin,
William Blyth,
Thomas Grindal.

At Mr. William Bikar's House.

William Bykar,
Math. Hawthorn and his wife,

Edward Pierce,
Nicholas Howfdon.

At Weynoack of Sir George Yeardley his people.

Nathaniel Elie,
John Flores,
Henry Gape,
—— Buckingham,
William Puffet,
William Walker,
John Gray,

James Boate,
John Suerfby,
Thomas Euans,
Thomas ap-Richard,
Henry Haynes,
John Blewet,
Henry Rice,

—— Hurt,
Jonas Alpart,
Thomas Stephens,
Samuel Goodwine,
John Snow and his
    Boy,
Margery Blewet.

At Powle-Brooke.

Capt. Nath. Powle, Efq., and his
    wife, Daughter to Mr Tracey,
Miftris Bray,
Adam Rayner's wife,
Barbara Burges,
William Head,

Thomas Woolcher,
William Meakins,
Robert ———,
Peter Jordan,
Nathanael Leydon,
Peter Goodale.

At Southampton Hundred.

Robert Goffe and his wife,
William Larkum,

John Dauis,
William Mountfort.

At Martin Brandons.

Lieutenant Sanders,
Enfigne Sherley,
John Taylor and his wife,

2 Boyes,
Mathew, a Polander.

At Captaine Spilman's House.

John Bafingthwayte,   Walter Shawe.

At Ensigne Spence his House.

William Richmond,   William Fierfax,
John Fowler,   The Tinker,
Alexander Bale,

Persons slaine at Martins-Hundred, some seaven miles from James-Citie.

Lieutenant Rich: Kean,   Richard Staples,
Mafter Tho: Boife &   his wife,
  Miftris Boife, his wife &   and Childe,
  a fucking Childe,   2 Maides,
4 of his men,   6 Men and Boyes,
A Maide,   Walter Dauies &
2 Children,   his brother,
Nathanael Jefferies wife,   Chriftopher Guillam,
Margaret Dauies,   Thomas Combar,
3 feruants,   A Man,
Mafter John Boife,   Ralphe Digginfon,
  his wife,   his Wife,
A Maide,   Richard Cholfer,
4 Men-feruants,   George Jones,
Laurence Wats,   Cifby Cooke,
  his Wife,   his wife,
2 Men feruants,   Dauid Bons,
Timothy Moife,   John Benner,
  his Man,   John Mafon,
Henry Bromage,   William Pawmet,
  his Wife,   Thomas Bats,
  his Daughter,   Peter Lighborrow,
  his Man,   James Thorley,
Edward How,   Robert Walden,
  his Wife,   Thomas Tolling,
  his Childe,   John Butler,
A child of John Jackfon,   Edward Rogers,
4 Men feruants,   Maximilian Ruffel,
Jofua Dary,   Henry, a Welchman.
  his wife,

At Mr. Thomas Pierce his House over against Mulberry Iland.

Mafter Tho: Pierce,
  his Wife,
  and Childe,

John Hopkins,
John Samon,
A French Boy.

At Mr. Edward Bennets Plantation.

Maſtter Th: Brewood,
  his wife,
  his Childe,
Robert Gray,
John Griffin,
Enſigne Harriſon,
John Coſtard,
Dauid Barry,
Thomas Sheppard,
Henry Price,
Robert ———,
Edward Jolby,
Richard ———,
Alice Jones,
Thomas Cooke,
Philip Worth,
Mathew a maid,
Francis Winder,
Thomas Conly,
Richard Woodward,
Humfrey Cropen,
Thomas Bacon,
Euan Watkins,
Richard Lewis,
Edward Towſe,

2 Seruants,
Thomas Ferris,
George Cole,
Remember Michel,
——— Bullocke,
Richard Chandler,
Henry Moore,
Nicholas Hunt,
John Corderoy,
Richard Cockwell,
John Howard,
Miſtris Harriſon,
Mary Dawks,
Annie Engliſh,
Rebecca ———,
Maſter Prowſe,
Hugh ———,
John ———,
Edward ———,
Miſtris Chamberlin,
Parnel a maid,
Humfrey Sherbrooke,
John Wilkins,
John Burton.

John Scotchmore, } Mᵣ John Pountis his men.
Edward Turner,

Edward Brewſter,   Lieutenant Pierce his man.

Thomas Holland,   Capt. Whittakers man.

At Master Walters his house.

Maſter Edward Walters,
  his wife,
  a Childe,

a Maid,
a Boy.

The whole number 347.

A BRIEFE DECLARATION

OF THE

PLANTATION OF VIRGINIA

DURINGE THE FIRST TWELVE YEARES, WHEN
SIR THOMAS SMITH WAS GOVERNOR OF
THE COMPANIE, & DOWNE TO THIS
PRESENT TYME.

BY THE

ANCIENT PLANTERS NOWE REMAINING ALIVE IN VIRGINIA.

1624.

PREFACE.

The next paper presented in this collection is a copy of the one from which Mr. Bancroft quotes in his introductory note to the meeting of the first Assembly, referring to it as "MS. in my possession." This is printed from the copy among the McDonald papers, and with its title and endorsements no intimation is given as to the date of its preparation, its author or authors, to whom it was addressed, or the use intended to be made of it. These questions are, however, answered almost entirely by reference to the entries in "Sainsbury's Calendar of State Papers," which, on pp. 65–'6, has the following: "1624. July. Petition of Gov. Sir Francis Wyatt, the Council and Assembly of Virginia to the King. Have understood that his Majesty, notwithstanding the unjust disparagement of the Plantation, has taken it under his especial care; intreat that credit may not be given to the late declarations presented to his Majesty concerning the happy, but indeed miserable, estate of the Colony during the first twelve years (of Sir Thos. Smythe's government), nor to the malicious imputations which have been laid upon the late government. Inclose the true state of both, and earnestly request that the present government may be continued. Pray that the King's tender compassion will not allow them to fall into the hands of Sir Thos. Smythe or his confidents." Signed by Sir Fran. Wyatt, Capt. Fan. West, Sir George Yeardley and eighty-six others. *Inclose.*— "Brief Declaration of the Plantation," &c., giving the whole title of this paper, verbatim, and a copious abstract of its contents. The earliest account of the horrors it relates is to be found in Smith's History, p. 105, in what is called "the examinations of Doctor Simons." This writer gives full details of the straits to which the Colonists were reduced and the expedients to which they resorted to appease hunger in 1609; adding, after the statements in regard to eating the Indian who had been buried several days and their eating "one another boyled, and stewed with rootes and herbes," the account of the man who "did kill his wife, powdered her, and had eaten part of her before it was known," and adding with a grim humour, "now whether shee was better roasted, boyled or carbonado'd, I know not, but of such a dish as powdered wife, I never heard of." His statements are copied, with more or less variation, by Beverley, Stith, Kieth and Burke, but not one of them go into the disgusting and improbable details named in the "Brief Declaration." Campbell also reports the stories, but adds, in regard to the wife murderer, "upon his trial it appeared that cannibalism was feigned to palliate the murder," p. 93. Neill quotes from the Records of the Virginia Company, "The Tragical Relation of Virginia Assembly," which was transmitted to England about 1621; this was intended as a reply to a petition of Alderman Johnson and others, who had represented to the King that the reports in regard to Sir Thos. Smith's management were false, and desiring an investigation. These petitioners were members of a faction which desired to break up the Virginia Company. In the Relation of the Assembly, Smith is charged with all the cruelties to the Colonists which are mentioned in this "Brief

Declaration"; torturing and starving to death being the punishments for minor offences; and asserting their confidence in the truth of these statements by concluding it with these words: "And rather to be reduced to live under the like gouernment we desire his Maties commissioners may be sent over wth authoritie to hange us." This is signed by thirty members of the General Assembly, including among the names, those of George Sandys, the poet, traveller and Secretary of the Colony, and Raph Hamor, the chronicler.—See Neill, pp. 407–411.

There is another reference to this starving time (as it is called) and its accompanying horror, which should not be allowed to pass without notice. As above stated, the worst state of affairs was reported to have existed in 1609, and in the next year a pamphlet with the following title was issued, "A true declaration of the estate of the Colonie of Virginia, with a refutation of such scandalous reports as haue tended to the disgrace of so worthy an enterprise. Published by aduise and direction of the Councell of Virginia. London, 1610." The writer of which, after referring to the slanders which had been circulated in regard to Sir Thos. Smith's government, and especially of the story of the wife-eater, says, "Sir Thomas Gates thus relateth the tragedie," and then follows a long passage to the effect that "one of the companie mortally hated his wife," and having killed her and secreted her body after cutting it into peices; when it was found out he said she died and he had hid her to satisfie his hunger, and had fed daily upon her, but upon searching his house they found a large quantity of provisions.—See Forcer tracts, Vol. III. The writers of the "Brief Declaration," and the "True Declaration," must have seen this statement published ten or twelve years before they wrote, and it is a little remarkable that they should have persisted in repeating a story which was far from being well authentitcated, especially as the true statement did not need this addition to increase the odium incurred by the mismanagement of Sir Thos. Smith, the evidences of which are herein set forth.

Stith reports the stories of the Indian "that had been slain and buried" being taken up and eaten, and "so did several others, one another that died," and also that of the man who "killed his wife and powdered her up, and eat the greater portion before it was discovered;" and adds, for many years after it was "remembered by the name of the *starving time*," p. 116–117. For many particulars nowhere else given, see Neill's History, pp. 407–411.

STATE PAPER OFFICE. ⎫
   COLONIAL.   ⎬
 Volume 3, No. 21, I. ⎭

A BREIFE DECLARATION *of the Plantation of Virginia duringe the first Twelve Yeares, when Sir Thomas Smith was Governor of the Companie, & downe to this present tyme. By the Ancient Planters nowe remaining alive in Virginia.*

WHERAS in the beginninge of Sir Thomas Smith's twelve yeares government, it was publifhed in printe throughout the Kingdome of Englande that a Plantation fhould be fettled in Virginia for the glorie of God in the propogation of the Gofpell of Chrift, the converfion of the Savages, to the honour of his Majefty, by the enlargeinge of his territories and future enrichinge of his kingdome, for which refpects many noble & well minded perfons were induced to adventure great fums of money to the advancement of foe pious & noble a worke, who have from the very firft been fruftrate of their expectation, as wee conceive, by the mifgovernment of Sir Thomas Smith, aiminge at nothinge more then a perticular gaine, to be raifed out of the labours of fuch as both voluntarilie adventured themfelves and were otherwife fent over at the common charge. This will cleerely appeare in the examination of the firft expedition & feverall fupplies in the tyme of his government.

The firft Plantation in Virginia confifted of one hundred perfons, fo flenderly provided for that before they had remained halfe a yeare in this new Collony they fell into extreame want, not havinge anything left to fuftein them fave a little ill conditioned Barley, which ground to meal & pottage made thereof, one fmale ladle full was allowed each perfon for a meale, without bread or aught elfe whatfoever, fo that had not God, by his great providence, moved the Indians, then our utter enemies, to bringe us reliefe, we had all utterlie by famine perifhed. How unable fo fmall a companye of people, foe poorely fent over, were to make way for fuch as fhoulde followe, may eafily be judged.

The firft fupplie beinge two fhippes, the John & Francis & Phenix, with one hundred & twenty perfons, worfe every way provided for then the former, arrived heere about eight or nine months after & found the Collony confiftinge of no more then forty perfons (of thofe) tenn only able men, the reft at point of death, all utterly deftitute of howfes, not one as yet built, fo that they lodged in cabbins & holes within the grounde; victualls they had none, fave fome fmall reliefe from the Indians, as fome yet living weare feelinge witneffes, neither were we for our future and better maintenance permitted to manure or till any grounde, a thing in a new Plantation principally to be regarded, but weare by the direction of Sir Thomas Smith, and his officers heere, wholly imployed in cuttinge downe of masts, cedar, blacke wallnutt, clapboarde, &c., and in digginge gould oare (as some thought) which beinge sent for England proved dirt. These works to make retorne of present proffit hindered others of more necessary consequence of Plantation.

After this first supplie there were some few poore howses built, & entrance made in cleeringe of grounde to the quantitye of foure acres for the wholl Collony, hunger & sicknefs not permitting any great matters to bee donne that yeare.

The second supplie was a ship called the Mary Margett, which arrived here nine months after, about the time of Michaellmas, in her sixty persons, most gentlemen, few or no tradesmen, except some Polanders to make Pitch, tarre, potashes, &c., to be retorned for present gaine, foe meanly likewise were these furnished forth for victualles, that in lesse then two monthes after their arrivall, want compelled us to imploye our time abroad in trading with the Indians for corne; whereby though for a time we partly relieved our necessities, yet in Maye followinge we weare forced (leavinge a small guarde of gentlemen & some others about the president at James Towne) to disperse the wholl Collony, some amongst the Salvadges but most to the Oyster Banks, where they lived uppon oysters for the space of nine weekes, with the allowance only of a pinte of Indian corne to each man for a week, & that allowance of corne continued to them but two weekes of the nine, which kinde of feeding caused all our skinns to peele off, from head to foote, as if we had beene flead. By this time arrived Captaine Samuell Argall in a small Barque, with him neither supplie of men nor victualls from the Company; but we understandinge that he had some small provisions of bread and wine, more then would serve his owne companie, required him and the master of the Barque to remaine ashoare whilst we might bring his sailes ashoare the better to assure us of his ship & such provisions as coulde be spared, whereunto he seemed willingly to condescend. Those provisions, at a small allowance of Biskett, cake, and a small measure of wine or beere to each person for a Daye some what relieved us for the space of a month, at the end of which time arrived the thirde supplie, called Sir Thomas Gates, his fleet, which consisted of seaven shippes & neere five hundred persons with whom a small proportion of victuall, for such a number, was landed; howses few or none to entertain them, so that being quartered in the open feilde they fell uppon that small quantitye of corne, not beinge above seaven acres, which we with great penury & sufferance had formerly planted, and in three days, at the most, wholly devoured it.

These numbers, thus meanly provided, not being able to subsist and live together weare soone after devided into three parties and disperfed abroad for their better reliefe. The firſt under commande of Captaine Francis Weſt to feat at the head of the River; a fecond under commande of Captaine John Smith, then Prefident, at James Towne, & the other, with Capt. John Martin, in the River at Nanfamun, which divifions gave occafions to the Indiens treacherouſly to cutt off divers of our men & boates, and forced the reſt at the end of fixe weekes, havinge fpent thofe fmall provifions they had with them, to retire to James Town & that in the depth of winter, when by reafon of the colde, it was not poſſible for us to endure to wade in the water (as formerly) to gather oyſters to fatisfie our hungry ſtomacks, but conſtrained to digge in the grounde for unwholefome rootes whereof we were not able to get fo many as would fuffice us, in refpect of the froſt at that feafon & our poverty & weakness, fo that famine compelled us wholly to devoure thofe Hogges, Dogges & horfes that weare then in the Collony, together with rates, mice, fnakes, or what vermin or carryon foever we could light on, as alfoe Toad-ſtooles, Jewes eares, or what els we founde growing upon the grounde that would fill either mouth or belly; and weare driven through unfufferable hunger unnaturallie to eat thofe thinges which nature moſt abhorred, the fleſh and excrements of man, as well of our owne nation as of an Indian, digged by fome out of his grave after he had laien buried three daies & wholly devoured him; others, envyinge the better ſtate of boddie of any whom hunger had not yet fo much waſted as there owne, lay waight and threatened to kill and eat them; one amonge the reſt flue his wife as ſhe ſlept in his bofome, cutt her in peeces, powdered her & fedd uppon her till he had clean devoured all partes faveinge her heade, & was for foe barbaroufe a fact and cruelty juſtly executed. Some adventuringe to feeke releife in the woods, dyed as they fought it, & weare eaten by others who found them dead. Many putt themfelves into the Indians' handes, though our enemies, and were by them ſlaine. In this extremitye of famine continued the Collony till the twenteth of Maye, when unexpected, yet happely, arrived Sir Thomas Gates & Sir George Somers in two fmall Barques* which they had built in the Sommer Iſlands after the wreake of the Sea adventure wherin they fett forth from Englande, with them one hundred perfons barely provided of vittel for themfelves. They founde the Collony confiſtinge then of but fixty perfons moſt famiſhed and at point of death, of whom many foone after died; the lamentable outcries of theirs foe moved the hartes of thofe worthies, not being in any forte able long to releive their wantes they foone refolved to imbarque themfelves & this poore re mainder of the Collonye, in thofe two pinnaces & two other fmall Barques then in the River, to fett faile for Newfoundland where they might releive their wants & procure one fafer paſſage for Englande. Every man, glad of this refolution, laboured his uttmoſt to further it,

* "The Deliverance, of 70 tonn, and the Patience, of 30 tonn." Letter from the Lord Delaware, Governor of Virginia to the patentees in England.— Introduction to Strachey's *Virginia Brittania,* p. xxiii.

fo that in three weekes we had fitted thofe barques and pinnaces (the beft we could) & quitted James Towne, leaving the poore buildings in it to the fpoile of the Indians, hopeinge never to retorne to re-poffefs them. When we had not failed downe the River above twelve miles but we efpied a boat which afterwards we underftoode came from the right Honourable Lorde La Ware, who was then arived at Point Comfort with three good fhipps, wherin he brought two hundred and fifty perfons with fome ftore of Provifions for them; but by reafon he founde the Collony in fo great want was forced to put both his owne people & the reft of the Collony to a very meane allowance, which was feven pounde of Englifh meale for a man a weeke, & five pounds for every woman, without the addition of any victuall whatfoever, except, in the ftead of meale, we took valuablie either peafe or oatmeale. Uppon the arrival of that boat, Sir Thomas Gates underftandinge from the Lord La Ware, that his Lordfhip was arrived with commiffion from the Company to be Govr & Capt. Genl of Virginia, & had brought men & provifions for the fubfiftinge & advancing of the Plantation, he the very next daye, to the great griefe of all his Company (only except Capt. John Martin), as winde and weather gave leave, retorned his whole company with charge to take poffeffion againe of thofe poore ruinated habitations at James Towne which he had formerly abandoned; himfelffe in a boate proceeded downeward to meete his Lordfhip who, making all fpeede up, arrived fhortly after at James Towne. The time of the yeare being then moft unfeafonable, by intemperate heat, at the end of June his people fuddenly fallinge generally into moft peftilent difeafes of Callentures and feavors, not leffe then one hundred & fifty of them died within few moneths after, & that chiefly for want of meanes to comfort them in their weak eftates. The refidue alfoe difabled by reafon of ficknes could performe nothing that yeare to the advance-ment of the Collony, yet with the help of thofe people which had ar-rived with Sir Thomas Gates, together with fome of the ancient Planters, who by ufe weare growen practique in a hard way of livinge, two fmall forts weare erected neare the rivers mouth at Kicoughtun, encompaffed with fmall younge trees, haveinge for houfing in the one, two formerlie built by the Indians & covered with bark by them, in the other a tent with fome few thatcht cabbins which our people built at our comming thether. We founde divers other Indian Howfes built by the natives which by reafon we could make no ufe of we burnt, killinge to the number of twelve or fourteene Indians, & poffeffinge fuch corne as we founde growinge of their plantinge. We remained there untill harveft, when we reaped (befides what we fpent) about the quantitie of one hundred and fiftie bufhells of corne, which, by order from the Lord La Ware, was tranfported to James Towne.

His Lordfhip intendinge to fend up certain forces to march to-wardes the mountaines for the difcoverie of gold or filver mines at the end of October, fent his Patents to Captaine Yardley and Captaine

Holcroft, commanders of thofe two forts at Kicoughtan, wherin his Lordfhip gave order that they fhould be forthwith abandoned & the people with all fpeede to be brought to James Citie, there to prepare for his intended march.

At that time there arrived a fmall fhip called the daintie, with twelve men & one woman, fome little provifion of victuall, two or three horfes & fome other flight neceffaries for the Collony. Soon after we fett forward for our intended march, havinge for our leaders Captaine Edwarde Brewfter & Captaine George Yeardley, being in number one hundred perfons, furnifhed with all fuch neceffary provifions, as the Collony at that time out of its poverty was able to provide. This defigne was hindered by reafon of the unfortunate loffe of all our chieffe men fkillfull in findeinge out mines, who weare treacheroufly flaine by the Salvadges (inviteinge them afhoare to eat victualls which they wanted) even when the meate was in theire mouthes, they careinge only to fill their bellies, forefaw not to prevent this danger which befell them.

This injury we revenged for the prefent (as we coulde) by killinge fome Indians and burninge many houfes, but by reafon of this difafter we proceeded not farther on our journey then the head of the River, where we fpent about three moneths doinge little but induringe much; his Lordfhip was there in perfon for the moft part of that time, but his difeafe of body groweinge much upon him he refolved to retire to James Towne, givinge order that the fort which we had built there fhoulde bee quitted and the troupe drawn downe, which accordingly was done. His Lordfhip then in regarde of his fickness was advifed to putt to Sea in his fhip, the Delaware, to feeke remedie in fome other parts for the health of his bodye. At his going he left Captaine George Percie Deputie Governor, the people (remaining under his command) provided for three months at a fhort allowance of victuals. The calamities of thefe times would not any way permit workes of great importance to bee performed, fith that we did was as much as we coulde doe to live and defende our felves.

The Plantations helde at his Lordfhips departure were only James Towne and Pointe Comforte, where was a fmall Fort fenced with Pallifadoes, in it one flight howfe, a ftore and fome few thatcht cabbins, which fhortly after by cafualtie was burnt with fire; fome few great ordinance were flenderlye mounted at James Towne and Pointe Comfort.

A fortnight after his Lordfhip's departure arrived a fmall fhip called the Hercules, with fome thirty people and fome provifions for them. The twelfe of May followeinge arrived Sir Thomas Dale with three fhips and three hundred perfons, his provifions for them of fuch qualitie (for the moft part) as hogges refufed to eat, fome whereof were fent backe to England to teftifie the fame, and that the reft was not better was juftified upon oath before the Hono^ble the Lorde Cheife Juftice of the Common Pleas, at Guilde hall in London, by Sir Thos. Gates & two other gentlemen.

Sir Thomas Dale, takinge into confideration the precedent times not to have fucceeded accordinge to the greedy defire of Sir Thomas Smith, prefently imployed the general Colony about the lading of thofe three fhips with fuch freight as the country then yealded, but a little before the fhips were readie to depart, Sir Thomas Gates arrived with three fhips and three carvills, with him three hundred perfons meanly provided with vidtualls for fuch a number. In this fleet, to our remembrance, arrived fixtie cowes and fome fwine; it was his care to dispatch thofe fhipps and carvills fraighted (as aforefaid) to the negledt of workes of greater importance. Sir Thomas Dale imediately uppon his arrival, to add to that extremitye of miferye under which the Collonye from her infancie groaned, made and publifhed moft cruell and tiranous lawes, exceeding the ftridteft rules of marifhall difcipline, which lawes were fent over by Sir Thomas Dale to Sir Thomas Smith by the hande of Mr. William Starchey,* then Secretarie to the State, and were retorned in print, with approbation, for our future government, as in divers bookes yet extant more fully appeareth.

At Michaellmas then next followinge, Sir Thomas Dale removed himfelf with three hundred perfons for the buildinge of Henrico Towne, where being landed he oppreffed his whole companye with fuch extraordinarye labors by daye and watchinge by night, as maye seeme incredible to the eares of any who had not the experimentall triall therof. Wante of houfes at firft landinge in the colde of winter, and pinchinge hunger continually bitinge, made thofe impofed labours moft infufferable, and the beft fruits and effedts therof to be noe better then the flaughter of his Majefty's free fubjedts by ftarveinge, hangeinge, burneinge, breakinge upon the wheele and fhootinge to deathe, fome (more than halfe famifhed) runninge to the Indians to gett reliefe beinge againe retorned were burnt to death. Some for ftealinge to fatisfie their hunger were hanged, and one chained to a tree till he ftarved to death; others attemptinge to run awaye in a barge and a fhallop (all the Boates that were then in the Collonye) and therin to adventure their lives for their native countrye, beinge difcovered and prevented, were fhott to death, hanged and broken upon the wheele, befides continuall whippings, extraordinary punifhments, workinge as flaves in irons for terme of yeares (and that for petty offences) weare dayly executed. Many famifhed in holes and other poore cabbins in the grounde, not refpedted becaufe ficknes had difabled them for labour, nor was their fufficient for them that were more able to worke, our beft allowance beinge but nine ounces of corrupt and putrified meale and halfe a pinte

---

* Mr. Strachey, sailed with Lord Delaware on the 1st of April, 1610, and arrived at the Capes on the 15th of May. He remained about two years. He left a well written manuscript account of his obfervations, with this title: "The Hiftorie of travaile into Virginia Brittania, * * * gathered and difcovered as well by thofe who went firft hither, as colledted by William Strachey, Gent., the firft secretary of the Colony;" which, edited by R. A. Major, Esq., of the British Museum, was published by the Hakluyt society in 1849.

of oatmeale or peafe (of like ill condition) for each perfon a daye. Thofe provifions were fent over by one Winne, a Draper, and Cafwell, a baker, by the appointment (as we conceave) of Sir Thomas Smith. Under this Tiranus Government the Collony continued in extreame flavery and miferye for the fpace of five yeares, in which time many, whofe neceffities enforced the breach of thofe lawes by the ftrictnefs and feveritye therof, fuffered death and other punifhments. Divers gentlemen both there and at Henrico towne, and throughout the wholl Collonye (beinge great adventurers and no trendes or alliance to Sir Thomas Smith) weare feeling members of thofe generall calamities, as far forth as the meaneft fellow fent over.

The buildings and fortifications of that Towne, or thereabouts, were noe way extraordinary, neither could want, accompanied with bloode and crueltie, effect better.

Fortification againft a foreign enemy there was none, only two or three peeces of ordenance mounted, and againft a domeftic noe other but a pale inclofinge the Towne to the quantitye of foure acres, within which thofe buildings that weare erected, coulde not in any man's judgement, neither did ftande above five yeares and that not without continuall reparations; true it is that there was a Bricke Church intended to be built, but not foe much as the foundation therof ever finifhed, but we contentinge our felves with a church of wood anfwerable to thofe houfes. Many other workes of like nature weare by him donne at Henrico and the precincts therof, but fo flightly as before his departure hence, he himfelf faw the ruine and defolation of moft of them.

Sir Thomas Gates likewife in his time erected fome buildinges in and about James Towne, which by continuall coft in repaireinge of them doe yet for the moft part in fome fort remaine.

A framed Bridge was alfoe then erected, which utterly decayed before the end of Sir Thomas Smith's government, that being the only bridge (any way foe to be called) that was ever in the country. At this time in all thefe labours, the miferye throughout the wholl Collony, in the fcarcitye of foode was equall; which penurious and harde kinde of liveinge, enforced and emboldened fome to petition to Sir Thomas Gates (then Governor) to grant them that favor that they might employ themfelves in hufbandry, that therby they and all others by plantinge of corne, might be better fed then thofe fupplies of victual which were fent from Englande woulde afforde to doe, which requeft of theirs was denied unleffe they woulde paye the yearlye rent of three barrels of corne and one monthe's worke to the Collonye, although many of them had been imployed in the generall workes and fervices of the Collony from the beginninge of the Plantation, which harde condition of Tenantfhip was then accepted rather then they woulde continue in thofe generall fervices and employments noe waye better then flavery. Moft part of the time that Sir Thomas Gates and Sir Thos. Dale governed we were at warre with the natives, fo that by them divers times were many of our people flaine, whofe blood Sir Thomas Dale neglected not to revenge, by divers and fundry executions, in killinge many, cuttinge downe and takinge away their corne, burninge their houfes, fpoiling their weares, &c.[*]

In this time alfoe the two fortes, fort Henry and fort Charles, at Kicoughton, were againe erected with fuch buildings as were formerly expreffed, not fortified at all againft a forreine enemye, and againft the Indian that common order of a pale or pallifadoe.

The fupplies fent out of Englande while Sir Thos. Gates and Sir Thos. Dale governed were thefe; a fmall barque called the John and Francis, which brought few men and lefs victual; the next a fmall fhip called the Sarah, with the like number of men and victuall; the next fhip called the Treforer, wherin came Capt. Samuell Argoll, bringinge with him to the number of fiftie good men, which fhip and men were wholly imployed in Trade and other fervices for relevinge of the Collonye; the next fhip, called the Elizabeth, with about thirteene perfons, for them little provifion; the next the fame Elizabeth came againe, with fome fmall ftore of provifions only; in her Sir Thos. Gates went for Englande, leavinge the government with Sir Thomas Dale.

A little before the departure of Sir Thomas Gates many of the ancient planters (by the inftigation of Sir Thomas Dale), uppon the promife of an abfolute freedome after three yeares more to be expired (havinge moft of them already ferved the Collonye fix or feaven yeares in that generall flavery) were yet contented to worke in the buildinge of Charles Citty and Hundred, with very little allowance of clothinge and victuall, and that only for the firft yeare, being promifed one moneth in the yeare, and one daye in the weeke from Maye daye till harveft, to gett our maintenance out of the earth without any further helpe; which promife of Sir Thos. Dale was not performed, for out of that fmall time which was allowed for our maintenance we were abridged of nere halfe, foe that out of our daily tafkes we were forced to redeeme time wherin to labour for our fuftenance, therby miferably to purchafe our freedome. Yet fo fell it out that our State (by God's mercy) was afterwardes more happie then others who continued longer in the aforementioned flaverye; in which time we built fuch houfes as before and in them lived with continual repairs, and buildinge new where the old failed, untill the maffacre.

For matter of fortification in all this time, were only foure peeces of ordinance mounted for our defence againft the natives. Soone after we weare feated at Charles Hundred, Sir Thomas Dales refolved of a journey to Pamonkey River, there to make with the Salvadges either a firme league of friendfhip or a prefent warre; they percieving his intent inclined rather for peace (more for feare then love) which was then

---

[*]"Their weares in which they take their fifh, which are certain enclofures made with reedes, and framed in the fafhion of a laborinth or maze, fett a fathome deepe in the water, with divers chambers or bedds, out of which the entangled fifh cannot returne or gett out, being once in.—Strachey, p. 68.

concluded betwixt them. That donne we retorned to our habitations, where great want and fcarcitye, oppreffed us, that continuinge and increafinge, (our firft harveft not yet being ripe) caufed in many an intended mutinye, which beinge, by God's mercy, difcovered, the prime actors were duly examined and convicted, wherof fixe beinge adjudged and condemned were executed.

After this, arrived for fupply a fmall fhip called the John and Francis, with about twenty perfons and little or noe provifions for them. The next fhip, called the Treforer, arived heere with the number of twenty perfons and as little provifions as the former, in which fhip after many other defignes were effected by Sir Thos. Dale, as makinge fpoile of the Kefchiacks* and Warifcoyacks, impaling fome necks of Lande, for defence againft the Salvadges, and in fifhing for our reliefe, &c., he departed from Virginia, and left the Government to Captain George Yardley, under whom the Collony lived in peace and beft plentye that ever it had till that time, yet moft part of the people for that yeare of his Government continued in the generall fervices followinge their labors as Sir Thos. Dale left them by order.

At Michaelmas followinge arrived a fmall fhip called the Sufan, her lading (beinge the firft Magazin) confiftinge of fome neceffarye provifions of clothinge, as our wants required, which goods were fould by Sir Thos. Smith's factor, as we fuppose, for a fufficient proffit, exchanginge with us their commodities for our Tobacco.

At Chriftmas then followinge, juft occafion beinge given by the Indians of Chiquohomini in many and feverall kindes of abufes, and in deridinge of our demandes, wherunto they had formerly agreed and conditioned with Sir Thomas Dale to paye us yearlye tribute, viz: a bufhell of corne for every Boweman, for which, by agreement, we were to give to each man one peece of copper and one iron tomahawke, and to the eight chiefe men each a fuit of redd cloth, which clothes and truckinge ftuffe we efteemed of more worth then their corne. Thefe and the like groffe abufes moved our Governor, Captaine George Yeardley, to levye a company of men, to the number of eighty-four, to bee revenged uppon thofe contemptuous Indians, which he, accordinge to his defire, fully executed, and returned home with the fpoile of them; concludinge, before his departure from them, a more firme league in appearance than formerly was, for that it continued unviolated almoft the fpace of two yeares; our people freely travelinge from Town to Towne (both men, women and children) without any armes, and were by the Salvadges lodged in their houfes, every way kindly intreated and noe way molefted.

In March followinge, our three yeares' time beinge expired, as it was our due, we of Charles Hundred demanded our long defired free-

---

* "Kifkiack (now Chescake—pronounced Cheesecake) on Smith's map is located on the south side of the Pamunck (now York) river about the site of Yorktown.—See Campbell, p. 66.

For Wariscoyack see note pp. 48, 49.

11

dome from that common and generall fervitude; unto which requeft Captaine George Yeardley, freely and willingly affented, to our great joy and comfort.   Yet remained the moft part of the Collony in the former fervitude; part of whom were farmers, the reft imployed in fuch workes as Sir Thomas Dale gave order for before his departure.

We that were freed, with our humble thankes to God, fell cheerfully to our perticular labours, wherby to our great comfort, through his bleffinge, we reaped a plentifull harveft.

In May followinge arived Captain Samuell Argoll with commiffion to be Governor.   He brought with him to the number of a hundred perfons, partly at the charge of the Company and partly at the charge of private adventurers; with them was brought a very little provifion for that nomber.   At his arrival heere he founde the Collony in all parts well ftored with corne, and at Charles Hundred a granery well furnifhed by rentes lately raifed and received from the farmers, which corne he tooke poffeffion of, but how it was imployed himfelfe can beft give an account.   Whileft he governed, the Collony was flenderly provided of munition, wherby a ftrict proclamation was made for reftraint of waftinge or fhooting away of powder, under paine of great punifhment; which forbiddinge to fhoot at all in our peeces caufed the loffe of much of oure corne then growinge uppon the grounde; the Indians perceivinge our forbearance to fhoote (as formerly) concluded thereuppon that our peeces were, as they faide, ficke and not to be ufed; uppon this, not longe after they were boulde to prefume to affault fome of our people, whom they flew, therin breakinge that league, which before was fo fairly kept.

Duringe his time of Government moft of the people of the Collony remained (as formerly) in the common fervice, their freedome not beinge to be obtained without extraordinary payement.

The next fhip that arrived heere was the George, fett forth, as we fupofe, at the charge of private adventurers, but came foe meanly provided with victuall, that had not we, the old Planters, relieved them moft of them had been ftarved.   The next fhips, called the Neptune and Treafurer, arived in Auguft followinge, fet out at the charge of the Right Honoᵇˡᵉ the Lord Laware, his noble affociates, and fome other private adventurers.   The people wᶜʰ arived were foe poorely victualled that had they not been diftributed amongft the old Planters they muft for want have perifhed; with them was brought a moft peftilent difeafe (called the Bloody flux) which infected all moft all the whole Collonye.   That difeafe, nothftanding all our former afflictions, was never knowne before amongft us.

The next fupply weare two fhips called the William & Thomas and the Guift, which arived in Januarie; the Guift beinge fett forth at the charge of the Societie of Martin's Hundred, the other by the Magazin and fome private adventurers.

The next, a fmall fhip called the Elinor (fett forth at whofe charge we know not), arived heere in Aprill after, and in her Capt. Samuell argoll, leaving his Government, fhipt himfelfe for Englande. Whatfoever els befell in the time of his Government we omit to relate, much beinge, uppon our oathes, alreadie fufficiently examined and our anfwers fent for Englande.

By all which hath heertofore beene faide concerninge this Collony, from the infancie therof and untill the expiration of Sir Thomas Smith's government, may eafily be perceived and plainly underftood what juft caufe he or any els have to boaft of the flourifhing eftate of thofe times, wherin fo great miferies and callamities were indured, and foe few workes of moment or importance performed, himfelfe beinge juftly to be charged as a prime author therof, by his neglect of providinge and alloweinge better meanes to proceede in fo great a worke, and in hindering very many of our frendes from fendinge much releife and meanes who beinge earneftly folicited from hence by our letters—wherin we lamentablie complained unto them—have often befought Sir Thomas Smith that they might have leave to fupplie us at their owne charge both with provifion of victuall and all other neceffaries, wherin he utterlie denied them fo to doe, proteftinge to them that we were in noe want at all, but that we exceeded in abundance and plentie of all things, fo that therby our frendes were moved both to defift from from fendinge and to doubt the truth of our letters, moft part of which weare by him ufually intercepted and kept backe; farther giveinge order by his directions to the Governor heere, that all men's letters fhould be fearched at the goinge away of fhips, and if in anye of them weare founde that the true eftate of the Collony was declared, they were prefented to the Governor and the indighters of them feverely punifhed; by which meanes noe man durft make any true relation to his frendes of his owne or the Collonye's true eftate; neither was it permitted to anye to have paffe to goe home, but by force were kept heere and employed as we have faide (fave fome few), one of whom received his paffe from the Kinge, and that clofely made up in a garter, leaft it fhould have been feized uppon and he kept heere notwithftandinge. Thofe whom their frendes procured their paffe in open courte from the Companye were, by private direction, neverthelefte made ftaye of, others procuringe private letters having been lett goe.

We muft alfoe noat heere, that Sir Thos. Dale, at his arivall finding himfelf deluded by the aforefaid protestations, pulled Capt. Newport by the beard, and threatninge to hange him, for that he affirmed Sir Thos. Smith's relation to be true, demandinge of him whether it weare meant that the people heere in Virginia fhoulde feed uppon trees.

Soe may we heere conclude, as fome have concluded for him, to what great growth of perfection (with the expence of that feaventie thoufand poundes) the Plantation was advanced in the time of his 12 years' government, but whether, as it is faide, he be to be praifed for the managaing of thefe affaires, with much unanimity, moderation, integritie and judgment, we leave it to cenfure.

At the end of this twelve yeares arived Sir George Yeardley to be Govr and founde the Collony in this eftate and thus furnifhed, vizt: For fortification againft a forreign ennemie there was none at all; two demy culverin only were mounted uppon rotten carriages and placed within James Citty, fitter to fhoot downe our houfes then to offend an ennemie. At Charles Hundred, which were mounted by Sir Thos. Dale, two demy culverin and one facre; fortifications againft a domes- tique enimie very mean. For Forts, Towns and Plantations he founde thefe: James Citty, Henrico, Charles Citty and Hundred, Shirley Hun- dred, Arrahattock, Martin Brandon and Kicoughton, all wch were but poorely houfed and as ill fortified; for in James Cittie were only thofe houfes that Sir Thom. Gates built in the time of his government, with one wherin the Govr allwayes dwelt, an addition beinge made therto in the time of Captaine Saml Argoll, and a church, built, wholly at the charge of the inhabitants of that cittie, of Timber, beinge fifty foote in length and twenty foot in breadth; at Pafpahayes alfoe weare fome few flight houfes built; at Henrico, two or three old howfes, a poore ruin- ated church with fome few poore buildings in the Ifland; Coxen Dale and the Maine and att Arrahatocke one houfe, at Charles Cittie fixe howfes much decayed, and, that we may not be too tedious, as thefe, foe were the reft of the places furnifht.

For people then alive about the number of foure hundred, very many of them in want of corne, utterlie deftitute of cattle, fwine, Poul- trie and other Provifions to nourifh them.

For Barques, Pinnaces, Shallops, Barges and Boates he founde only one olde Frigott, which belonged to the Sommer Iflandes, one olde Shallopp built in Sir Thos. Dale's time, one boat built in Sir Sam'l Ar- goll's time, with two fmall boates belonginge to private men. For mu- nition a very fmall quantitye, the moft part thereof beinge very bad and of little ufe. For minifters to inftruct the people he founde only three authorized, two others who never received their orders.

For ftaple commodities at his arrivall he founde none afoot fave only Tobacco. The natives he founde uppon doubtfull termes, neither did we ever perceive that at any time they voluntarilie yealded them- felves fubjects or fervants to our Gracious Soveraigne, neither that ever they tooke any pride in that title, nor paide they at any time any yearly contribution of corne for the fuftentation of the Collony, nor could we at any time keepe them in fuch goode refpect or correfpond- encie that they and we did become mutuallie helpfull or proffitable, each to other, but to the contrary, whatfoever at any time was done uppon them proceeded from fear without love, for fuch help as we have had from them have been procured by fworde or trade. And heere can we noe way approve of that which hath lately beene faide in the behalfe of Sir Thos. Smith, by fome of his new frendes, that a flourifhinge plantation in Virginia, erected in the time of his 12 yeares government, hath fince been diftroyed through the ignorance of fucceedinge Governors heere, for that by what we have already faide all the worlde may judge in what a flourifhinge eftate it was, and to what growth of perfection it was advanced, at the arivall of Sir Geo. Yeardley to be Govr here, it beinge then in our judgements, that were members of the colony, in a poore eftate.

The whole 12 yeares expired.

Aprill, 1619.—Arived Sir Geo. Yeardeley, bringing certain commiffions and inftructions from the Company for the better eftablifhinge of a Commonwealth heere, wherin order was taken for the removing of all thofe grievances which formerly were fuffred and manifefted the fame by publifhinge a Proclamation that all thofe that were refidend heere before the departure of Sir Thos. Dale fhould be freed and acquitted from fuch publique fervices and labours which formerly they fuffered, and that thofe cruell lawes by which we had foe longe been governed were now abrogated, and that we were now to be governed by thofe free lawes which his Ma^{ty's} fubjects live under in Englande. And farther that free libertie was given to all men to make choice of their dividents of lande and, as their abilities and meanes w^d permitt, to poffeffe and plant uppon them. And that they might have a hande in the governinge of themfelves, it was granted that a general affemblie fhould be helde yearly once, wherat were to be prefent the Govr and Counfell with two Burgeffes from each Plantation freely to be elected by the inhabitants thereof; this affembly to have power to make and ordaine whatfoever lawes and orders fhould by them be thought good and proffittable for our fubfiftance. The effect of which proceedinge gave fuch incouragement to every perfon heere that all of them followed their perticular labours with fingular alacrity and induftry, foe that, through the bleffinge of God uppon our willinge labors, within the fpace of three yeares, our countrye flourifhed with many new erected Plantations, from the head of the River to Kicoughtan, beautifull and pleafant to the fpectators, and comfortable for the releife and fuccor of all fuch as by occafion did travaile by land or by water; every man giveinge free entertainment, both to frendes or others. The plenty of thefe times likewife was fuch that all men generally were fufficiently furnifhed with corne, and many alfoe had plenty of cattle, fwine, poultry and other good provifions to nourifh them. Monethly courtes were held in every precinct to doe juftice in redreffinge of all fmall and petty matters, others of more confequence beinge referred to the Govr, Counfell and Generall Affemblie. Now alfoe were begunne and fett a foote the erectinge of Iron Workes, plantinge of vines and mulberrie trees for the nourifhinge of filke wormes; a trial made for filke graffe tillage for Englifh graine, gardeninge, and the like, which gave great hopes of prefent and future plenty in their feverall perticulars,

wherin no doubt but much more had been effected had not great ficknes and mortalitie prevented.

Thofe yeares fallinge out to be generally contagious through
this continent, the people alfoe fent over arrived heere at the moft unfeafonable time of the yeare, beinge at the heat of Sommer, and divers
of the fhips brought with them moft peftilent infections, wherof many
of their people had died at Sea, foe that thefe times alfoe of plenty
and libertie were mixed with the calamities of ficknes and mortalitie.

In October, 1621, Arived Sir Fras. Wyatt, Knight, with commiffion
to be Govr and Capt. Genl of Virginia. He ratified and confirmed all
the afore mentioned liberties, freedomes and priveledges, to our great
happines and content; the country alfoe flourifhed and increafed in
her former proceedinges, as iron workes, plantinge of vines and mulberrie for filke, &c. A fhip alfoe was fent to the Summer Iflandes
for fuch commodities as that place afforded, as Potatoes, Fig Trees,
Orange and Lemon Trees, and fuch like, many of which profper and
growe very likely to increafe. But amidft this happines was the Hande
of God fett againft us, in great part, no doubt, for the punifhment of
our ingratitude in not being thankefull but forgettfull that by his mer-
cye we were delivered from fuch bondage and calamitie as before time
we had fuffered. Juftly likewife were we punifhed for our greedy de-
fires of prefent gaine and proffit, wherin many fhowed themfelves in-
fatiable and covetous; we beinge too fecure in truftinge of a treacherous enimie, the Salvadges, they, whileft we entertained them frendley
in our houfes, tooke their opportunities and fuddenly fell uppon us,
killing and murdering very many of our people, burninge and devaft-
inge their houfes and plantations, this happeninge uppon the *two and
twenteth of March* followinge (1622), ftroocke fo at the life of our well-
fare by blood and fpoile, that it almoft generally defaced the beautie
of the wholl Collonye, puttinge us out of the way of bringinge to perfection thofe excellent workes wherin we had made foe faire a beginninge.

This deadly ftroake being given to the great amazement and ruine
of our State, caufed our Governor and Counfell, withall fpeede, for the
fafetie of the reft (left the Indians fhoulde take courage to purfue what
they had begunne), to re-collect the ftraglinge and woefull Inhabitants,
foe difmembered, into ftronger bodies and more fecure places. This
enforced reducement of the Collony into fewer bodies, together with
the troble of warre then in hande, caufed the year following a flender
harveft to be reaped, wherby we weare conftrained to relye upon hopes
for our reliefe by fhippinge out of Englande, and by trading with the
more remote Salvadges, moft part of which fupplies from Englande
unfortunately mifcarried by the waye, the Salvadges, likewife, from
whome we hoped to have helpes by trade, proved our moft treacherous
ennemies, cunninglye circumventinge and cruellie murderinge fuch as

were employed abroade to gett reliefe from them, by all which mifacci-
dents we fell that yeare into great want and fcarcitye; which fince, by
the bleffinge of God, through our fupplies we have had from the Company, together with a plentifull harveſt, hath bene abundantly reſtored.
Our Govʳ , Counfell and others have ufed their uttermoſt and Chriſtian
endeavours in profequtinge revenge againſt the bloody Salvadges, and
have endeavoured to reſtore the Collonye to her former profperitye,
wherin they have ufed great diligence and induſtrye, imployinge many
forces abroade for the rootinge them out of feverall places that therby
we may come to live in better securitie, doubtinge not but in time we
fhall clean drive them from thefe partes, and therby have the free
libertie and range for our cattle, the increafe of whom may bringe us
to plentie, and maye alfoe more freely goe on againe with fetting up
thofe ſtaple commodities which we hoped by this time to have brought
to good perfection.

For the fupplies of fhippinge, men, cattle and provifions that have
arived heere fince Sir Thomas Smith left his government we can not
nowe well reckon up, they beinge manye, but muſt referre you to the
printed bookes and to the Liſts and Invoices retorned by Sir Geo.
Yeardley.

For the State of the Collony at this prefent we leave to the report
of fuch commiffioners as are nowe fent over by the Right Hon. the
Lordes of his Maᵗⁱᵉ'ˢ privie counfell.

This being reade in the Genˡ Affemblie received full approbation.

[Endorfed.]
Virginia—A relation of its Planting.

[This document is undated but is placed in the Callendar among
papers of 1625?]

A LIST

OF THE NUMBER OF

MEN, WOMEN AND CHILDREN

INHABITING IN THE SEVERAL COUNTIES

WITHIN THE COLONY OF VIRGINIA,

ANNO D^{NE}, 1634.

PREFACE.

The three succeeding papers are printed from the De Jarnette collection. The first is a census in gross without any details of sex, age or social condition. In these respects it lacks the interest which one feels in the list made out in 1623.

In February, 1623, there were living in the Colony 1277 persons, and including 371 who had died during the preceding year, i. e. since April, 1622; it is evident that the greatest number of inhabitants during the year ending February 16, 1623—not including those murdered in the the the massacre—amounted to 1648; and in 1634, eleven years afterwards, they amounted to 5,119, being an increase of 3,471, or an average of about 315 per annum, by birth and immigration. Accustomed as we are to the rapid growth of new countries this seems but a small increase, but when it is remembered that they made the voyage in sailing vessels only, and that it then not unfrequently lasted three or four months, we have little cause for wonder.

The next paper is a copy of a letter from His Majesty Charles II., to the Governor, Sir Wm. Berkeley, returning his thanks for a present of silk grown in Virginia. The first settlers were very anxious for success in this department of industry, and the House of Burgesses in 1657–'8 passed a law offering a premium of 5,000 pounds of tobacco to any one who made "100 pounds of wound silke in any one year," and in the next session, 1658–'9, the premium was made 10,000 pounds of tobacco for 50 pounds of "wound silke." We have frequently heard repeated a tradition to the effect that Charles II. wore a robe made of Virginia silk at his coronation. The circumstance of which this document is evidence, is probably the nearest approach to any thing of the sort that ever occurred, and hereafter this with the foolish and groundless story of one of the Lees going to see him when an exile at Breda, to offer him a crown and a refuge in Virginia, must be consigned to that oblivion which is likely, soon, we hope, to receive many of the mythical legends which have heretofore passed current for the history of Virginia.

The third is a list of the parishes and their ministers in 1680, the number of the latter showing that the people were poorly provided for in this respect, and that some of the parishes had no ministers. This deficiency was, however, in a measure provided for by the appointment of " readers " under the operation of acts passed February 1632–'3, by which if a minister's curé " is so large that he cannot be present on the Saboth and other holy days. *It is thought fit* That they appoint deacons for the reading of common prayer in their absence;" and further, in March, 1661–'2, it was enacted " That every parish not haveing a minister to officiate every Sunday doe make choice of a grave and sober person to read divine service at the Parish church."—Hen. Vol. I., p. 208 ; Vol. II., p. 46, 54.

STATE PAPERS,
   COLONIAL.
Vol. 8, No. 55 (1634).

A LIST *of the number of men, women and children Inhabitinge in the severall Counties w*th*in the Collony of Virginia. Anno D*^{ne}*, 1634.*

Imprimis, from Arrowhattock to Shirley hundred Iland, on both fides the river, being within the Countie of Henrico,	419
Item, from Shirley hundred Iland to Weyfnoake, on both fides the River, being wthin the countie of Charles Citty,	511
Item, from Upper Cheppeake Creeke to Lawnes Creeke on the Southward fide, and from Checohominey River to Creeke on the northward fide of the River, being wthin the Countie of James Citty,	886
Item, from Ketche's Creeke & Mulbury Iland to Maries Mount, on the northward fide of the river, being wthin the countie of Warricke river,	811
Item, from Lawne's Creeke to Warrofquyoake Creeke on the fouthward fide of the river, beinge within the Countye of Warrofquyoake,	522
Item, from Maires Mount to Fox hill, wth the Plantations of the Back river & the old Pocolfon river on the Northward fide, and from Elizabeth river to Chefepeake River on the fouthward fide of the river, being wthin the Countie of Elizabeth Citty,	859
Item, in the Plantations of Kifkyake, Yorke & the new Pocolfon, being within the Countie of Charles River,	510
Item, in the Plantations on the Efterlie fide of Cheffepeake Bay, being wthin the Countie of Accowmack,	396
The whole number is,	4,914

After this lift was brought in there arrived a fhip of Holand with 145 from the Bermudas.

And fince that 60 more in an Englifh fhipp wch likewife came from the Bermudas.

I certify that the foregoing is a true and authentic copy taken from the volume above named.

JOHN McDONAGH,
Record Agent,
July 14th, 1871.

A LETTER

FROM

His Majesty, Charles the Second,

To SIR WM. BERKELEY, Gov. of Va.

ACKNOWLEDGING THE RECEIPT OF A PRESENT OF
SILK MADE IN THE COLONY, AND PROMISING
HIS PROTECTION TO THIS BRANCH
OF INDUSTRY.

1648.

STATE PAPERS,
COLONIAL—VIRGINIA.
Vol. 59, No. 115, (Nov'r —, 1668).

[Partly damaged by damp.]

Trusty & welbeloved, Wee Greet you well. Wee have received wth much content y^e dutifull refpects of that Our Colony in ye prefent lately made us by you & ye Councell there of ye firft product of ye new Manufacture of Silke, w^ch, as a mark of Our Princely acceptation of yor dutyes & of y^r particular encouragement, Wee refolve to give to yor induftry in ye profecution and improvem^t of that or any other ufefull Manufacture, Wee have comanded to be wrought up for ye ufe of Our owne perfon, and herein Wee have thought good to   *   *   *
  *   *   ledge from Our owne Royall   *   *   *   *   *   you of Our more efpeciall care & protection in all occafions that may concern that our ancient Colony and Plantation, whofe laudable induftry, rayfed in good part & improved by ye fobriety of ye governm^t , we efteeme much, & are defirous by this & any other feafonable expreffion of Our favor, as farre as in us lies, to encourage. And foe Wee bid you Farewell. Given at Our Court at Whitehall, the — day of November, in ye 20th yeare of our Reigne, 1668.

By his Matie's Comand.

His Ma^ty to S^r W^m. Berkeley & Colony.

[Endorfed.]

To our Trufty and Welbeloved Sir William Berkeley, Kn^t, Our Governour of our Colony of Virginia, to be communicated to y^e Councill of that Our Colony.

I certify that the foregoing is a true and authentic copy taken from the volume above named.

JOHN McDONAGH,
Record Agent,
July 1ft, 1871.

A LIST

OF

THE PARISHES IN VIRGINIA

In 1680.

STATE PAPERS,
COLONIAL—VIRGINIA.
Vol. 60, No. 410 (June 30th, 1680).

A LIST OF THE PARISHES IN VIRGINIA.

JUNE THE 30TH, 1680.

Henrico County	Varina, ½ Briftol,*	} John Ball.
Charles Citty Co^ty	½ Briftol, Jordan, Weftover, Weyonoak, Martin Brandon,	Readers onely. Mr Paul Williams.
Surry County	Southwork, Lawns Creek,	Mr John Clough. Mr John Woyre.
James Citty County	Martins hundred, ½ Brewton, James Citty, Wallingford, Wilmington,	Mr Rowl^d Jones. Mr Thomas Hampton.
Ifle of Wight	Ifle of Wight Parifh, Lower Parifh,	Mr Robt Park. Mr Wm Houfden.
Nanzemund	Upper Parifh, Lower Parifh, Chicokatuck Parifh,	Mr John Gregory. Mr John Wood. Mr Wm Houfden, who ferves in Ifle of Wight alfoe.
Warwick County	Denby, Mulberry Ifland,	Mr John Larwence for both.
Eliz. Citty County	Inone Parifh.	Mr John Page.
Lower Norfolk	Eliz. River Parifh, Lynhaven Parifh,	Mr Wm Nern. Mr James Porter.

*The ½ occurs in such cases as when one portion of the parish is in one county and the other portion in another. Thus Bristol parish was partly in Henrico and partly in Charles City counties.

Yorke County	½ Brewton, Hampton Parifh, York Parifh, New Towfon Parifh,	Mr Rowland Jones. Mr Edwd. Foliott. Mr John Wright.
New Kent	South fide. North fide, St. Peter's Parifh, Bliffland Parifh, St. Steven's Parifh, Stratton Majr,	Mr Wm. Sellick. Mr Tho. Taylor. Mr Wm. Williams. Mr Robt. Carr.
Gloftr County	Kingfton, Ware Parifh, Telfoe Parifh, Abingdon,	Mr Michaell• Zyperius. Mr —— Clark. Mr Thomas Vicars. Mr John Gwynn.
Middx County	Chrift Church Parifh,	Mr John Sheppard.
Rappa County	Farnam, Sydenburn,	Mr Charles Davies. Mr —— Dudley.
Stafford County	Stafford Parifh, Choatanck,	John Wough.
Weftmerland County	Copeland Parifh, Wafhington,	Mr —— Scrimmington. Mr William Butler.
Northumberld Cou'ty	Fairfield, Wacacommico,	Mr John Farnefold. Mr Davies, who ferves alfoe at Farnam.
Accomack County	Accomack Parifh,	Mr Henry Parkes.
Northampton County	Northampton Parifh, Hungers Parifh,	Mr Thomas Teagle.
Lancafter County	Chrift's Church, White Chapple,	Mr Benj. Doggett.

I certify that the foregoing is a true and
authentic copy taken from the volume
above named.
JOHN McDONAGH,
Record Agent,
July 14th, 1871.

ADDENDA.

The following additions to the text and notes are suggested as explanatory, without being considered superfluous.

Page 16.—" The sixte petition, to change the sauage name of Kicowtan," was granted. In 1621, Treasurer Sandys in his report to the Company informed them that the name had been changed to Elizabeth Cittie.—Neill's history, page 178.

Page 25.—The word " howes " inserted in connection with various kinds of dogs, is our modern word hoe; Smith has it hows on page 86, and howes on page 162.

Page 29.—Capt. Henry Spelman, was the third son of the distinguished antiquary, Sir Henry Spelman, of Conghan, Norfolk, England. He was about twenty-one years of age when he came to Virginia, in 1609, for which he accounts as follows : " Beinge in displeasuer of my frendes, and desirous to see other countryes. After three months' sayle we cum with prosperus winds in sight of Virginia." Afterwards he says, " I was carried by Capt. Smith, our President, to ye Fales, to ye litell Powhatan, wher, vnknowne to me he sould me to him for a towne called Powhatan."—Spilman's Relation, pp. 15, 16. Dr. Simons, in Smith's General Historie, says : " Captain West and Captain Sickelmore sought abroad to trade; Sickelmore, upon the confidence of Powhatan, with about thirty other as careless as himselfe, were all slaine; onely Jeffrey Shortridge escaped, and Pokahontas, the King's daughter, saued a boy called Henry Spilman, that liued many yeeres after, by her meanes, among the Patawmokes;" this occurred in 1609.—Smith, p. 105. He remained with the Indians but little more than one year, for in 1610 Capt. Argall being sent to the " riuer Patawmoke to trade for corne," where finding him, used Spelman's influence to secure the loading of his vessel with corn, and Spelman returned with him to Jamestown.—Smith, p. 108. Spelman adds, " a id brought into England," p. 221. We then lose sight of him until he is arraigned before the Assembly at Jamestown in 1619 (ante p. 29) He makes his final appearance in 1623, when we are told, he was sent with a bark and twenty-six men to "trucke in the River Patawmek," where at some place, the name of which was to his companions unknown, he landed with twenty-one of his companions, when the savages made hostile demonstrations " and presently after they" (the five left in the bark) " heard a great brute amongst the Saluages ashore, and saw a man's head thrown downe the banke, whereupon they weighed Anchor and returned home, but how he was surprised or slaine is vncertaine."—Smith p. 161. Spelman wrote a short account of his observations while among the Indians, and it laid in obscurity until the sale of Dawson Turner's library, in 1859, when it was bought by Mr. Joseph Lilly and, by accident, again lost; and at the sale of Mr. Lilly's library, in 1871, it was again discovered and purchased for James F. Hunniwell, Esq., who has had one hundred copies printed for private circulation.

Spelman was not the only Englishman with the savages. In the same year that Spelman was sold for a town, or saved by Pocahontas—whichever version being correct— Admiral Newport gave Powhatan a boy, named Thomas Salvage, in exchange for " Namontack, his trustie seruant." Spelman says Savage was murdered by the Indians, but there is a tradition that he lived nearly all his life with them; became possessor of a tract of land on the eastern shore by gift and that it remained in his family until within the last ten years, when it was sold by some of his descendants then living in Philadelphia. The authority for this statement is obtained in correspondence with Hon. Hugh B. Grigsby, LL. D., President of the Virginia Historical Society.

Page 39.—To note to Jordan's Journey it may be added that a reference to this place is doubtless made when Smith says: " After the massacre many of the inhabitants fortified themselves against other attacks, and Master Samuel Iorden gathered but a few about him at Begger's Bush" (the title of one of Fletcher's comedies) " where he fortified."—Smith, p. 150; Campbell, p. 164.

Page 47.—The following may be added to the note on Glass House: " For glass they," the Indians, " knowe not, though the country wants not sal-sodiack enough to make glasse, and of which we have made some store in a goodly house sett up for the same purpose, a little without the island where Jamestown stands."—Strachey's Virginia Brittania (1612), p. 71. " To take care of Capt. Wm. Norton and certaine Italians sent to sitt a glass house."—Instructions to Sir Francis Wyatt (1621), Hening I., p. 116.

Page 47.—To note on Warwick-Squrake add: " In the autumn of 1607, Capt. Smith, with " six or seaven in company," went to Kicoughtan to get food from the Indians by trade. On his return he discovered the town and county of Warraskoyack."—Smith, page 45.

Richmond, Va., *July* 15, 1874.